D0637290

Classic
HORSE STORIES

Classic
HORSE STORIES

Edited and with an Introduction
by
STEVEN D. PRICE

THE LYONS PRESS
GUILFORD, CONNECTICUTT
AN IMPRINT OF THE GLOBE PEQUOT PRESS

Copyright © 2002 by The Lyons Press

ALL RIGHTS RESERVED. No part of this book may be
reproduced or transmitted in any form by any means,
electronic or mechanical, including photocopying and
recording, or by any information storage and retrieval
system, except as may be expressly permitted by the
1976 Copyright Act or in writing from the publisher.
Requests for permission should be addressed to The Globe
Pequot Press, PO Box 480, Guilford, CT 06437.

The Lyons Press is an imprint of
The Globe Pequot Press

Printed in the United States of America

10 9 8 7 6 5 4 3 2

Design by Claire Zoghb

Library of Congress Cataloging-in-Publication
data is available on file.

Also By The Author

TEACHING RIDING AT SUMMER CAMP (The Stephen Greene Press, 1972)

PANORAMA OF AMERICAN HORSES (Westover/ Crown, 1973)

CIVIL RIGHTS, Vols. 1 & 2 (Facts On File, 1973)

GET A HORSE!: Basics of Backyard Horsekeeping (Viking, 1974)

TAKE ME HOME: The Rise of Country-and-Western Music (Praeger, 1974)

THE SECOND-TIME SINGLE MAN'S SURVIVAL HANDBOOK, with William J. Gordon Praeger, 1975)

OLD AS THE HILLS: The Story of Bluegrass Music (Viking, 1975)

HORSEBACK VACATION GUIDE (The Stephen Greene Press, 1975)

SCHOOLING TO SHOW: Basics of Hunter-Jumper Training, with Anthony D'Ambrosio, Jr. (Viking, 1978)

THE WHOLE HORSE CATALOG, Editorial Director (Simon & Schuster, 1979, revised 1985, 1993, 1998)

RIDING'S A JOY, with Joy Slater (Doubleday, 1982)

ALL THE KING'S HORSES: The Story of The Budweiser Clydesdales (Viking, 1983)

THE BEAUTIFUL BABY NAMING BOOK (Simon & Schuster, 1984)

RIDING FOR A FALL (Tor Books, 1988)

THE POLO PRIMER, with Charles Kauffman (The Stephen Greene Press, 1989)

THE ULTIMATE FISHING GUIDE (HarperCollins, 1996)

CAUGHT ME A BIG 'UN, with Jimmy Houston (Pocket Books, 1996)

THE COMPLETE BOOK OF THE AMERICAN QUARTER HORSE (The Lyons Press, 1998)

TWO BITS' BOOK OF THE AMERICAN QUARTER HORSE (The Lyons Press, 1999)

ESSENTIAL RIDING (The Lyons Press, 2000)

THE ILLUSTRATED HORSEMAN'S DICTIONARY (The Lyons Press, 2000)

Contents

Introduction

The Lyons Press's invitation to compile yet another horse-related anthology made my spirits soar like a caprioling Lipizzaner. Like its predecessors, THE QUOTABLE HORSE LOVER and THE GREATEST HORSE STORIES EVER TOLD, this project would send me off on a literary round-up. I'd work my way through my own and others' bookshelves, then corral and cull examples of the world's best equestrian writing (as the man said with a smirk, it's a dirty job but somebody's gotta do it).

There was, however, one ground rule: All fourteen selections had to be classics in the sense of having some age on them. Nothing more recent than, say, World War Two. Otherwise, everything was fair game.

A piece of cake, I thought, and it was. Some choices didn't take me very far from my own library. *Black Beauty* and *National Velvet* practically jumped off the shelf, and rightly so, because these classics continue to appeal to generation after generation of readers.

National Velvet serves as evidence that the British equestrian literary tradition before the Second World War was almost exclusively foxhunting and racing. From the many possibilities came "Philippa's Fox Hunt" from *Experiences of an Irish R.M.* (some TV viewers may remember it from a "Masterpiece Theatre" adaptation of several decades ago), an equally charming account of steeplechase racing from World War One poet Sigried Sassoon's *Memoirs of a Foxhunting Man*, and "The Man Who Hunts And Doesn't Like It" from Anthony Trollope's Hunting Sketches.

A diversion: The Trollope selection that appears here narrowly nosed out the hunting scene in his novel *The Eustace Diamonds*, but there were many other candidates from which to choose. The author's works provide an embarrassment of equestrian literary riches. That's because Mr. T was a passionate foxhunter, and in ways that made him something of a folk hero in my eyes. According to his autobiography, he spent most of his literary career writing from 5:00 to 8:00 in the morning before going off to his "day" job as a postal inspector . . . except for those mornings when he hunted. That is to say, anyone who would put his job on the back burner in favor of going riding certainly had his priorities straight!

In a far less sporting playing-for-keeps vein is "Sensations of a Cavalry Charge," Winston Churchill's you-are-there recollections of mounted warfare. And included as another evocative example of British literary equestrian heritage is H. H. Munro's "Esme."

Although Australian poet "Banjo" Paterson is better known for his minor epic poem "The Man From Snowy River," included here is his rollicking account of "The Geenbung Polo Club."

Our own country's history is well served by several selections: "The Round-Up," Theodore Roosevelt's pre-presidential account of life as a cowboy, and Mark Twain's encounter with the Pony Express from "Roughing It." Taken together, they provide a panoramic view of the Old West and a taste of reality that is miles away from the glamour of Hollywood sugarcoating.

Although the rest of the selections may not fit into more specific categories, they more than hold their own in such distinguished company. Witness the other-worldly narrative of Charles Tenny Jackson's "The Horse of Hurricane Reef," Wilber

Daniel Steele's mystery story "Blue Murder," and "The Chimera," Nathaniel Hawthorne's retelling of the Greek legend.

And then there's Leo Tolstoy's "Strider—The Story Of A Horse," of which I first heard when a colleague mentioned that, "one of the Russian writers wrote a short story about a horse from the horse's perspective." That was the good news. The not-so-good news was that he couldn't remember the name of the author.

What was a compiler to do? The answer, as most questions can be answered these days, was found on the Web. "Hmm, Russian short story writer..," I mused, then entered "Chekhov+horses" in a search engine.

No luck, so I tried "Tergenev+horses." The search came up with an anecdote that bears repeating:

Tolstoy himself once estimated that he had spent seven years of his life in the saddle. A fellow writer, Ivan Turgenev, once observed Tolstoy whispering to a mangy old nag the two had encountered on a walk in the country. "I could have listened forever," Turgenev later wrote. "He had got inside the very soul of the poor beast and taken me with him. I could not refrain from remarking: 'I say, Leo Nikolayevich, beyond any doubt, you must have been a horse once yourself.'"

"Ah-hah," I thought and tried "Tolstoy+horse." The result if the remarkably touching tale with which this volume concludes.

STEVEN D. PRICE

NEW YORK, NY

SEPTEMBER 2002

"My Breaking In"
from Black Beauty

[ANNA SEWELL]

I was now beginning to grow handsome; my coat had grown fine and soft, and was bright black. I had one white foot and a pretty white scar on my forehead. I was thought very handsome; my master would not sell me till I was four years old; he said lads ought not to work like men, and colts ought not to work like horses till they were quite grown up.

When I was four years old Squire Gordon came to look at me. He examined my eyes, my mouth, and my legs; he felt them all down; and then I had to walk and trot and gallop before him. He seemed to like me, and said, "When he has been well broken in he will do very well." My master said he would break me in himself, as he should not like me to be frightened or hurt, and he lost no time about it, for the next day he began.

Everyone may not know what breaking in is, therefore I will describe it. It means to teach a horse to wear a saddle and bridle, and to carry on his back a man, woman, or child; to go just the way they wish, and to go quietly. Besides this he has to learn to wear a collar, a crupper, and a breeching, and to stand still while they are put on; then to have a cart or chaise fixed behind, so that he cannot walk or trot without dragging it after him; and he must go fast or slowly by just as his driver wishes. He must never start at what he sees, nor speak to other horses, nor bite, nor kick, nor have any will of his own; but always do his master's will, even though he may be very tired or hungry; but the worst of all is, when his harness is once on, he may neither jump for joy nor lie down for weariness. So you see this breaking in is a great thing.

I had of course long been used to a halter and a headstall, and to be led about in the fields and lanes quietly, but now I was to have a bit and bridle; my master gave me some oats as usual, and after a good deal of coaxing he got the bit into my mouth, and the bridle fixed, but it was a nasty thing! Those who have never had a bit in their mouths cannot think of how bad it feels; a great piece of cold hard steel as thick as a man's finger to be pushed into one's mouth, between one's teeth, and over one's tongue, with the ends coming out at the corner of your mouth, and held fast there by straps over your head, under your throat, round your nose, and under your chin; so that no way in the world can you get rid of the nasty hard thing; it is very bad! Yes, very bad! At least I thought so; but I knew my mother always wore one when she went out, and all horses did when they were grown up; and so, what with the nice oats, and what with my master's pats, kind words, and gentle ways, I got to wear my bit and bridle.

Next came the saddle, but that was not half so bad; my master put it on my back very gently, while old Daniel held my head; he then made the girths fast under my body, patting and talking to me all the time; then I had a few oats, then a little leading about; and this he did every day till I began to look for the oats and the saddle. At length, one morning, my master got on my back and rode me round the meadow on the soft grass. It certainly did feel queer; but I must say I felt rather proud to carry my master, and as he continued to ride a little every day I soon became accustomed to it.

The next unpleasant business was putting on the iron shoes; that, too, was very hard at first. My master went with me to the smith's forge, to see that I was not hurt or got any fright. The blacksmith took my feet in his hand, one after the other, and cut away some of the hoof. It did not pain me, so I stood still on three legs till he had done them all. Then he took a piece of iron the shape of my foot, and clapped it on, and drove some nails through the shoe quite into my hoof, so that the shoe was firmly on. My feet felt very stiff and heavy, but in time I got used to it.

And now having got so far, my master went on to break me to harness; there were more new things to wear. First, a stiff heavy collar just on my neck, and a bridle with great side-pieces against my eyes called blinkers, and blinkers they were, for I could not see on either side, but only straight in front of me; next, there was a small saddle with a nasty stiff strap that went right under my tail; that was the crupper. I hated the crupper; to have my long tail doubled up and poked through that strap was almost as bad as the bit. I never felt more like kicking, but of course I could not kick such a good master, and so in time I got used to everything, and could do my work as well as my mother.

I must not forget to mention one part of my training, which I have always considered a very great advantage. My master sent me for a fortnight to a neighboring farmer's, who had a meadow which was skirted on one side by the railway. Here were some sheep and cows, and I was turned in among them.

I shall never forget the first train that ran by. I was feeding quietly near the pales which separated the meadow from the railway, when I heard a strange sound at a distance, and before I knew whence it came—with a rush and a clatter, and a puffing out of smoke—a long black train of something flew by, and was gone almost before I could draw my breath. I turned and galloped to the further side of the meadow as fast as I could go, and there I stood snorting with astonishment and fear. In the course of the day many other trains went by, some more slowly; these drew up at the station close by, and sometimes made an awful shriek and groan before they stopped. I thought it was very dreadful, but the cows went on eating very quietly, and hardly raised their heads as the black frightful thing came puffing and grinding past.

For the first few days I could not feed in peace; but as I found this terrible creature never came into the field, or did me any harm, I began to disregard it, and very soon I cared as little about the passing of a train as the cows and sheep did.

Since then I have seen many horses much alarmed and restive at the sight or sound of a steam engine; but thanks to my good master's care, I am as fearless at railway stations as in my own stable.

Now if anyone wants to break in a young horse well, that is the way.

My master often drove me in double harness with my mother, because she was steady and could teach me how to go better than a strange horse. She told me the better I behaved the better I should be treated, and that it was wisest always to do my best to please my master; "but," said she, "there are a great many kinds of men; there are good thoughtful men like our master, that any horse may be proud to serve; and there are bad, cruel men, who never ought to have a horse or dog to call their own. Besides, there are a great many foolish men, vain, ignorant, and careless, who never trouble themselves to think; these spoil more horses than all, just for want of sense; they don't mean it, but they do it for all that. I hope you will fall into good hands; but a horse never knows who may buy him, or who may drive him; it is all a chance for us; but still I say, do your best wherever it is, and keep up your good name."

The Horse of
Hurricane Reef

[CHARLES TENNEY JACKSON]

The mares are for whoever is man enough to take them," retorted Jean Abadie from the bow of the barge which the towing launch was shoving into the mud shoal on the bay side of Île Dautrive. "Rojas has given them up. The white stallion killed his son, Emile, four years ago. No man of the camps around here will land on this reef; he has a name, that wild white devil!"

"You see, M'sieu Lalande, it is not stealing," added Pierre as he stopped the motor and looked at the stranger in the stern seat.

"It is stealing," grunted Joe Lalande, "else why do we come under cover of storm to rope the colts and mares? Well, no matter. Once we get them aboard and up to the Mississippi plantations, I will show you something, you shrimp-seine Cajuns. Throwing a rope, eh? Over westward they never yet showed me a horse I could not break."

The two seine-haulers from Sanchez's platform looked at him doubtfully. "Over westward," to the men of Barataria Bay, began at the dim marsh shore and stretched to infinity. A native never ventured so far; out there anything might be possible. But no man had faced the exiled king of Dautrive reef. Pierre muttered again how they would get the young mares—they would first shoot the white stallion. It was the hurricane month; they knew well enough that an obliterating sea would come this week over the dunes and marshes. Old Rojas, living with his grandchildren, orphaned by the white brute's savagery, on the far west point of the island, would never know what happened to the five mares and colts. More than once the gale off the Gulf had left the shell-beached *chenaies* far up the bay strewn with the dead cattle of the people of the reefs.

The big Lalande laughed as he followed through the salt grass to the first low dunes. "Shoot him! You'll shoot no horse with me! You say he's so bad; show him to me! I'll rope and load him, too, my friends, or he will finish me. If we lift Rojas's animals we take 'em all."

The Cajuns laughed in nervous disbelief. Lalande, a native also, who had returned this season to haul seine in Sanchez's company, might have been a great man with the pitching broncos he told of, but Rojas's great white stallion—well, this boaster would see! The brute would allow no seine crew to land on the Île Dautrive; they told of his charging upon the fishing skiffs clear out to the surf line. Sanchez, the boss, had shot him once as he fled to his lugger, leaving the bleeding stallion to rend and trample an abandoned seine.

Grand-père Rojas, in his camp across the shoal depression that cut through the reef, had never tried to reclaim the wild mares and the colts of the white stud's breed. The generations of them lived on the coarse reef grass and the rain pools; an oysterman had no use for horses, anyhow. His son, Émile, had tried this foolish experiment of raising horses on the reef, and given his life under the stallion's hoofs. *Grand-père* had shrugged and let the breed go wild; yet, as Lalande muttered when Jean and Pierre proposed to use his skill in lifting the younger animals, the horses were his to the scrawniest colt. But Lalande had come. He would show the shrimpers; and even if they only roped and dragged the least unruly one to the barge, Lalande could break them and Pierre sell them on the plantations. Yet it was horse stealing. Lalande would not gloss that over, but something else had drawn him here—the stories the islanders told of the white stallion's savagery.

"Old Rojas's son, I will be the avenger," he grunted, sullenly, and came on the day Pierre had chosen for the secret raid.

Abadie had stopped on the sandy trail broken through the mangroves to the top of the sand ridge. "*Bon Dieu!*" he whispered, pointing. "His track, Lalande! Big as a bucket! *Eh bien*! I'd rather face a hurricane than this white tiger!"

Lalande had stepped out in the open sand patch. From here the dunes fell sway to the Gulf beach. Already the sea was rising. Between Dautrive and the outer bar curious, oily currents were twisting in unwonted directions, and beyond them the surf broke in white, serried teeth gleaming against the black southeast. The sky was ribboned in black lines streaming northerly; the wind came in fitful smashes against the mangrove thickets and then seemed sucked up to howl in the writhing clouds.

"There'll have to be quick work," muttered Pierre. "I tell you this is bad, this sea. We waited too long, M'sieu Lalande. We better be back across the bay, and try for the colts another time."

Lalande's gray eyes narrowed surlily. He straightened his powerful figure above the wind-slanting bushes. The two other raiders had crept back through the brush. It was disconcerting to find the animals crossing their trail behind. "If he smells a man he will never let up on us, Lalande," muttered Jean. "Kill him, then!"

The white leader had crossed the trail of the raiders. He turned, broke through the brush, and gained the ridge forty yards from them. Lalande could see him now against the black skyline very plainly. A tremendous brute towering above the others, his shaggy mane flowing backward in the wind, his muzzle outstretched, his neck tensed until the powerful muscles bulged the satin skin. He was suspicious; he stood there, a challenging figure to the storm, but his eyes were roving watchfully into the thickets as a tiger scenting prey.

Lalande glanced back. His comrades had slunk below the mangroves. They were brave, hardy men of the hurricane coast, but the evil name of the sea horse of Île Dautrive seemed to hold them nerveless. The horse was coming on along the top of the ridge, slowly crashing through the brush with alert glances right and left. His pink nostrils quivered, his iron-gray tail raised and swept in the wind puffs.

"They will shoot," muttered Lalande. "If he trails them the cowards will shoot." And he stepped more in the open, and then shouted, "Come, thieves, let the colts go! I will need you on the throw-line to check and choke this brute!" Breast-high in the windswept thickets, he was laughing and coiling his rope. This was a foe for a strong man who boasted!

The great horse suddenly upreared with a neigh that was like the roar of a lion. No man had so much as ever put a finger on him; he had beaten the brains from one, broken the leg of another, and smashed two seine skiffs in the shallows for invaders. He had been the lord of the reef. Now he reared again and again as he plunged through the mangroves watching for the fugitives as a cat would a mouse under a flimsy cover of straw.

His satiny flanks were toward Lalande; apparently he had not yet discovered the man behind him in this hunt for the others. And then, out of pure panic as the white stallion broke near him, Jean Abadie fired. Lalande cursed and sprang down the slope of dunes after him. He knew he would need their help when he roped this horse; it was no starveling cayuse of the Texas range. But he saw now that the two islanders were skulking for the boat in the last fringe of the mangroves. They would never make it; out in the open the white stallion would crush them both ere they covered half the marsh grass, unless, indeed, they killed him.

The brute saw them now; he swerved in a tremendous rush below the man on the higher sand. Lalande was whirling his rope, and when he heard the hiss of it through the air he laughed, for he knew the throw was true.

"*Eh, bien,* devil! You and me!" He went down sprawling, seeking a root of the tough mangroves to snub the line. He caught one, then it was jerked out; and he went trundling and rolling over and over through the sands hanging to the lariat. He might as well have roped a torpedo. The horse was in the open now rearing and bucking, but with his savage eyes still on the fugitives. They were floundering through the water. Jean was jerking the mooring lines from the barge, and Pierre poling the launch back from the swamp grass. The stallion was surging on with the line cutting deep in his neck, but they could not see this in the welter of spray he threw in his charge.

Joe Lalande was on his back in the high grass, bruised and dizzy from his ride on the throw-rope. It was lying out taut through the grass; and for a time the man did not stir. The stallion was plunging somewhere out there, still implacable with fury to get at the shrimpers. Then, Lalande heard the first throb of the motor. They were getting away, leaving him, then? They must think him killed—a good end for a braggart who would rather fight the stud than steal the mares!

He lay in the grass listening, without even resentment. The wide reach of the bay northward was

flecked with white surges rising between those curious, oily bulges of water, the first stir of the creeping tides which come upon the Gulf shores before
the hurricane winds. Lalande remembered enough
of his boyhood among the island folk to know that.
Pierre was right; they had waited too long for this
week of storm to raid Rojas's wild horses.

He crept around on the jerking line. Above the
grass billows he saw the brute. He was whirling
madly in the shallows fighting this strange, choking
clutch on his neck. Then he charged back up the
dunes, and Lalande barely had time to lie out on the
end ere he was dragged again. But when the stallion
plunged into the thickets, no human strength could
hold. He felt his fingers breaking in the tangle of
rope and roots, his face ground into the sand and
pounded by showers of sand from the brute's hoofs.

Lalande staggered to his feet presently, cleared his
eyes, and followed a crashing trail over the sand
ridge. Northward he saw the launch rocking its way
across the pass with whiplike streamers of wind hitting the water beyond. Everywhere the coast folk
would be debating whether to quit their platform
camps and take to the luggers or trust to the oaks of
the *chenaies* and their moorings. The hurricane
month, and a sea coming up past Cuba! Île Derniere
had vanished under the waves; La Caminada gone
with six hundred souls; these were traditions of the

coast, but the natives knew what a hurricane tide meant on the low, loose sand islands that fringed the Louisiana swamps.

Lalande paused on the highest ridge. There was that sullen glisten of the sea, cut through with patches of white, and the green-back horizon gaping to east and west and blotting out with gray squalls. The great wind had not come yet beyond these first squadrons. The big man shrugged as he regarded it. The hurricane tide was shoving frothy fingers out over the shoals. Across the sandy stretch westward he could just see the shack camp of *Grand-père* Rojas on the highest ridge of Dautrive. A few ragged oaks showed white against the sky. The old man ought to be leaving with his orphaned grandchildren, taking his stout oyster lugger and making for the solid land fourteen miles north across the bay.

"It is no place for little ones," muttered Lalande in the Cajun patois. These people never will leave quick enough before the storms. I can see the old man's lugger still riding behind the point. He is a fool, Old Rojas, afraid to put foot on this end of the reef because of the white stud, but stubborn against the sea which comes like a million white horses."

He went warily on the crushed trail. That throw-rope would foul somewhere in the mangroves; that stallion would choke himself to a stupor, for not all the strength in the world can avail against lungs bursting for air. Then he saw the mares. They were huddled in a hollow of the dunes, the colts about them as if confused, uncertain, their shaggy coats ruffled in the wind. That wind was moaning now, high and far; not so bad here on the reef, but striking in slants on the sea as if the sky had opened to let an arrow loose. A hundred miles away as yet, that Gulf hurricane wind, but mounting; sixty, eighty, a hundred miles an hour—a hundred and twenty-five in the bursts that presently drove the sand dunes into smoke.

The rim of wet sand beyond the dry, hummocky space was covered with sheets of black water racing from the surf line, breaking on the shoals.

And here Lalande saw what he had sought. There was the white mound in the ripples. With a cry he dashed for it. The horse was down. He had not thought it would come so soon. But the end of the trailing rope had fouled a great drift heap, and the brute had kept on charging and fighting until he choked and fell in the first wash of the sea. The slip-noose was bound to cut him down if he kept on hurling his weight against it, Lalande knew.

He wished he had seen the last magnificent fight against it on the sands; but now he walked quickly around the fallen brute, and knelt to touch his distended, quivering nostrils. The eyes were shut but bulging under a film. The great sides were heaving, a rumbling groan found escape somehow; it was as if the mighty heart was breaking with a last throb against this mysterious power choking its strength away.

"Eh, soldier!" whispered Lalande, and felt high on the horse's neck.

A sudden apprehension took him. Perhaps the thong had killed the renegade? He did not mean that; he was filled with a great exultant joy in this savage. He had stalked and subdued him alone! He stood above this outstretched, trembling body in the first sea ripples, laughing.

"Come, boy! The fight's not done yet! Not the end yet." He twisted his fingers into the taut rope, forced on the dragging driftwood, and eased the tension bit by bit. The rope was buried in the white skin; he worked hurriedly, fearing it was too late.

"Come, come; this will not do—" he was whispering into the stallion's tense ear, fighting at the rope. Then came a fierce, convulsive blow, an explosive sigh, a struggle, and the stallion lay quiet again. He was breathing in great, resurging sighs. His filmed eyes opened slowly. Lalande kept patting his muzzle while he hitched the noose into a knot that would not choke again. He did not know why he did this, only it seemed fair. He was looking close into the brute's eyes which were beginning to glow with sense again; and to withdraw the choking hitch seemed only justice.

Lalande stood up and looked down at the white stallion. The water was roaring out there now. The skyline was blown white as feathers. The mangroves were slanting; and he suddenly realized that the wind was hard as a plank against his cheek. Not bursting, but steadily lying against the land. There was no rain, yet the air was full of water streaming in white lines through a growing darkness.

"Get up!" he shouted. "The sea is coming. This is no place to be! Comrade, on your feet!"

And the great horse did so. First plunging up, but with his haunches squatted in the water as he looked slowly about. Then to all fours and standing with his tail whipped about on his heaving flanks. He seemed watching that wall of blow water from the Gulf. Watching steadily, undaunted. The sands under the racing froth seemed trembling; one could hardly see the mangrove dunes not a hundred yards away.

Lalande swiftly turned his eyes from the ridge at a sound. It had seemed a shriek above the tumult. Then he leaped, and the wind appeared to lift him above the shaking earth.

For the great stud was on him. Upreared above him, a shaggy hoof coming not an inch's breadth from his skull.

Just a glimpse of those red, savage eyes; and the impact of those huge feet almost upon his own. Then Lalande ran. The hurricane wind flung him onward, but he could hear the rush of the white stallion. The entangled rope checked the charge only enough to allow the man to hurl himself into the first mangroves, crawl under them in a whirl-wind of rising sands, and keep on crawling. When he stopped, he knew the horse was crashing in the thickets hunting him. He saw him as a wraith against the sky, plunging his head low enough to ferret out his enemy, blowing explosively and hurl-ing the tough mangrove clumps aside.

Lalande kept on his stealthy crawl. He lay, finally, in a water-riven dusk under the lee of the dunes, lis-tening. "*Dieu!*" he panted. "I said, a soldier! The hur-ricane could not stop that hate of men!"

For half an hour he did not move. The brute had lost his trail. And when Lalande crawled to the top of the dunes he could not stand. All over the weather side the sea had risen. It was white. White, that was all he could say. And the wind? It did not seem a wind, merely a crushing of one's skull and lungs. When he tried to turn away it threw him headlong, but he got to his feet on the northerly, lee side of the sand ridge and fought on.

The sand was dissolving under his feet, and now he saw the water of the bay streaming by him. The inner marshes were gone; the hurricane tide was on, and sixty miles inland it would rush to batter on the cypress forests and the back levees of the plantation lands. Lalande had no illusions about Île Dautrive—he had been a lad on this coast—but he kept on, for the highest ridge was at the western point. Across the sand shoal, beyond this point, was still higher land, a clay fragment in which grew a few stout oaks. By these Old Rojas's camp had stood. It did not stand there now, thought Lalande. Nothing built by man on the reef would stand. *Grand-père* and the children of the man whom the white stallion had killed must certainly have taken to the lugger—escaped before the hurricane tide rushed upon the flimsy shack. Surely, yes. Rojas was no fool!

Lalande kept on, clinging to the thickets when the worst clutch of the wind was on him. The roaring of it all was so steady that actually he seemed in a great silence, as if a new element had enveloped him—a normal thing, this shock and unceasing tenseness of feeling and of sound. Through it he strode steadily himself, a strong man with neither fear nor curiosity—a mere dull plunge on to the last foothold of that reef which was churning to gruel behind his steps. He could not miss the point; there was no other spot to reach, and the hurricane was guide as well as captor.

And his mind was upon the lord of Dautrive Island. "He will go. Perhaps he is gone now. And the mares and colts, all off the reef by now." And a grim satisfaction came that the white stud had turned on him at the last. It was fine to think of. The savage had not cringed. "I do not want anything that can be stolen," he murmured, and spat the sea spray from his sore lips. "His mares and colts, he fights for them—that devil!"

And he began shouting profane, fond challenges and adulations to his conqueror somewhere in this white chaos of a night. A whipping wisp of scud was that charging shape above the torn thickets; any single shriek of the storm, his trumpeted challenge in return. Lalande boasted to his soul that he was seeking his foe; if it was the last stroke of his hand he wished it raised to taunt the white, oncoming devil.

Even the storm glimmer had faded when he felt the water shoaling from this armpits to his waist. This was the west point, the highest, and here, with hands locked to the stoutest of the mangroves, he would have to let the sea boil over him as long as a strong man could—then go.

On the western high point at last, and nothing to see, nothing to feel but the submerged bushes and the earth dissolving so that he had to keep his feet moving to avoid each becoming the center of a whirlpool.

"It is a storm," Lalande grunted. "Two white dev-
ils on this reef." He remembered seeing spaces of
mirrored calm, peaceful coves over which they told
him orange trees had bloomed in cottage yards of
the reef dwellers. The sea had devoured the islands
in a night, dug the hole, and lain down in it like a
fed tiger. Lalande, crowded closer to the stouter
thickets, put out his hand in the dark. He touched a
wet, warm surface, heaving slightly.

The skin of a brute. He smoothed the hair in the
rushing water, felt along. A wall of steely flesh broadside to the tidal wave. Lalande softly slipped his hand
over the huge round flank. The water was swirling
about them both to the man's armpits now. Lalande
knew. They were on the highest point, but ahead lay
the shoal pass. The sea was eating away this point;
what was left was sinking, flicked off into the meeting currents around Dautrive and swept inland. The
island would be silt on some cane planter's back fields
forty miles up the Mississippi delta within the week.

But for the last of his domain the lord of Dautrive
was fighting with his last foothold. The white devil
of the sea was doing what man could not do. Lalande laughed in the blackness. The stallion could
not feel his soft touch in all that beating welter of
sand and debris churning around him. He rested his
arm across the unseen back—the brute would think
it was a driftwood branch. The man stepped for-

ward. There was no other foothold now, it seemed. He reached his hand to the shoulder, up to feel the stiff, wet mane. He laughed and patted the bulged muscles.

"We go, you and I," he grumbled. The mangroves were slatted out on the tide rush, tearing loose, reeling past them. "Eh, friend? The last—"

And then he knew that the horse had whirled, upreared in the blackness with a scream of fury. Lalande sprang to the left, into deep, moiling water.

He felt the plunge of his foe just missing him once more. But another body struck him and then was whirled off in the meeting tides. He collided with a colt in the dark; and now he guessed that the white stallion's breed had been gathered on the refuge shielded to the last by his huge bulk against the inexorable seas.

They were gone now. There was no more foothold on Dautrive either for the exiles or the man who had come to subdue them. Lalande knew he must not go with the tidal wave. It was death anywhere out there. The water would rush fifty miles inland over the battered reefs. So he fought powerfully back to get a handhold on the mangrove thickets through a whirlpool of dissolving sand.

But the man could not breast those surges through the dark; he felt himself driven farther back in a tangle of foam and debris, and suddenly came a whiplike tightening about his legs. He was dragged under and out across the current until he fought down to grasp this thing that had him.

It was his throw-rope, the new and heavy line he had brought to conquer the white stud that the island men feared. Lalande plunged up and along it. The rope was tight and surging athwart the drift. When he got his head above water he knew he was clear of the disintegrating sand point, overwhelmed by the rollers in the pass and stung by the spray, but moving.

An unseen guide, a mighty power was drawing aslant the inshore tide. Lalande hauled along until he felt the rhythmic beat of the stallion's stroke; along until he touched his flank. When he could put his hand to his long mane, Lalande laughed. He hung there, and felt the brute plunge higher at this contact. Once, twice, and then the stud settled to his fight.

The lord of Dautrive could not shake him off or rend him with teeth or hoof. He was being ridden through the blackness and the sea.

Lalande began shouting. He could not resist the impulse of defiance; the great horse had been merciless to him on the island, so now he howled at him whenever he could keep the salt water from his teeth.

"*Eh, bien*! Big fellow, you see I am here! If you go, I go! Lalande is with you—devil! Fight! Fight on; a man is on your back at last. A last ride, too, white devil!"

For he had no hope of anything except to be battered to a pulp by the drift logs and wreckage in the
pass or drowned over the flooded marshes. But the
stallion would not give to the northward tide; always he kept fighting to windward and westerly.
When he plunged on these tacks Lalande swung out
straight over his back, but clinging lightly and calling his taunting courage to the brute.

"The west ridge," muttered the rider. "He knows
that, the oaks and the clay soil. If anything hangs together in this sea it will be that." So he clung in the
dark. Nothing but the incessant battles of the horse's
broadside in the hurricane tide kept that feeling in
Lalande's heart that the swimmer was trying to cross
the pass to Rojas's oak grove. The white devil was
blind in the white sea, but he remembered that. Lalande could feel the leg strokes steady and true even
when the waves lifted or buried them, or when they
were half drowned in the whipped foam among
patches of reef wreckage. The man was fighting at
this debris to keep it from the stallion's neck when
he felt something else streaming along his flanks. It
appeared to be submerged bushes or thick, long
grass twisting about beneath them. And there was a
changed note to the hurricane's tumult.

Lalande swung up on the stallion's back, listening.
The swells of the pass were slower here, huge and
strangling, but not with the fierce rush they had

battled. The horse was swimming more to seaward, almost head on now, and once he arose as if his forefeet had struck the earth.

"He has found the marsh," muttered Lalande. "Night of wonders; nothing else!"

Still that powerful, steady stroke under the man's clinging limbs. The brute was seeking whatever land might be above the water. Then Lalande began to think, as again he felt the forefeet touch bottom.

"Then we fight again, eh, tiger? Shake me off and come at me! Make the oaks and we'll see!"

The horse plunged past a torn oak stump which smashed him in the side. He was in water to his withers, but Lalande knew he was climbing. He got a foothold, leaned against the tide rushing through the oak grove, and kept on. Against the man and the horse there crushed another trunk, denuded of leaves, swinging by its roots, staggering them with its blows. The sea was over this also, Lalande knew. If it came higher there was no hope here.

Then the stallion stopped. He stood belly deep in the lee of another oak trunk which Lalande could feel in the utter dark. And the man sat silent astride the white king of Dautrive who had lost his domain and his subjects. He moved his legs across the heaving flanks—a sort of stealthy challenge. He wanted the white stud to know that he, Joe Lalande, was there astride him. He laughed and leaned to pat the unseen arch of the neck.

And then again came that furious, uprearing plunge of the great brute. His head came about in a side blow, his teeth tearing at Lalande's face as the rider swerved out under this twisting, maddened attack. He heard that trumpet cry again of the wild horse seeking him as he dragged himself about the oak tree in the water. He stood clutching the rope, trying to make out the brute's form.

Then he knew that the swells riding through the twisted oaks were slowed; the yelling of the winds more fitful, higher; and a sort of check came to the clutch on his body against the tree. Lalande seemed to stand in a frothy eddy as if the sea had stopped running and was foaming to an apex about him. And he knew what it meant, the moment that always comes in the Gulf hurricanes. The wind was dying off and changing. The sea could do no more. It had piled its flood as far inland and as high as even its strength could hold. Its whirling center was now over the coast, the wind whipping fitfully, now southwest, westerly, northward, and beginning to rise again. But there came one moment when it was almost a calm, silence except for that roaring in the sky.

"*La revanche,*" muttered the man. "Now comes the worst—the rush of the tide back to sea. The good God help them all, these Cajuns who have not found refuge up the bay. *La revanche*—that is when they die!"

He felt about his oak trunk, wondering if it were still rooted firmly. The white stallion must be just about the torn branches, for Lalande still had the trailing line. And then came something that numbed him with uncanny fear. A voice out in the dark, a child's cry among the oaks.

"*La revanche*! *Grand-père,* it is coming! Get the lines the other way, *Grand-pére*—"

Lalande went plunging toward the spot. "*Nom de Dieu*! It is not possible? Rojas!" He shouted, and stumbled among wreckage of trees and timbers around his waist. "Rojas, you are in the grove?"

A dim light glowed behind a blanket. He saw a boy had snatched this moment of the falling wind to try the lantern. When Lalande waded to the spot an old man straightened up on the other side of a sunken raft. Upon it, under the blankets, were lashed the forms of Rojas's children, the orphans of Emile, who had once sought to tame the white horse of Île Dautrive. Old Rojas held the lantern close to his white beard. He seemed as frightened as was the small boy by the stranger's coming.

Old Rojas had been trying to spike a cross-piece to his shattered raft. His lugger had been smashed in the first reach of the hurricane, and he had torn up the planks of his camp floor to build this refuge anchored to the biggest oaks of the grove. They knew what to do, these Cajuns of the reefs, when they were caught by the hurricane tide. Cut the mast from the lugger and drift inland, seize an anchorage before the dreaded *revanche* took them seaward; or if not that, hang to one's oak stumps!

Lalande did not waste the precious moments with a single question.

"A brave fight, old man. I see you made a brave fight! Give me your raft-lines. The other way around now, and to the stoutest trees. This sea, it is like a mad tiger when it has to go back defeated! Come." He took the mooring-line and plunged off in the waist-deep froth.

"Day of wonders!" mumbled Old Rojas. "A man on the reef—living. A big man, strong after the hurricane! It is impossible!" He went hammering his raft as it surged and plunged by his shoulders, ordering the youngster to make himself fast once more in the life ropes which held them all to the shaking planks. There was no whimper from the four children. They raised big dark eyes, staring from *Grand-père* to the strange man who was battling back in the first seaward rush of the waters to make them fast against *la revanche*. The wind was smiting again. It appeared to fall out of the blackness to the north, blast after blast, rising swifter, smiting the piled-up waters, hurling them over the reef islands with thrice the speed they had come in.

The dim lantern went out. The fugitives tied themselves on again. If the worn lines held and the raft kept together they might live. "Name of Names!" grumbled Old Rojas. "A man coming to us out of the sea? He said he would make fast for us. If not, my children—well, we must trust him."

Lalande had struggled off into the new rush of the wind with the raft-lines. They were frayed and ragged. He made them fast to his own throw-rope. He would get this rope off the stallion somehow, and make it fast to the big oak. If not—he shrugged, well, then, nothing! Every wreck of a lugger, plank of a camp, drift log, tree, that was loose would be miles in the open Gulf tomorrow to eddy endlessly in *la revanche*.

The old man's mooring-lines would not reach the big oak. Lalande had thought that, combined, they might last the night out, but the sea and wind were whipping fast on him in the dark. He had to plunge out shoulder deep to the tree, feeling of his line.

"The white devil is there and quiet," he grumbled. "If he would let me slip the rope from his shoulders and tie it to the tree!" He breasted the brimming tides over the submerged isle past the oak, his hand cautiously out to the dark. "Devil!" he called softly. "This is for Emile Rojas's young ones.

The rope, devil! We've fought, you and I, but now let me have it."

The line was tight past the oak stump. The weight of the raft was already coming strongly on it as the tide began to seethe through the shattered grove. Lalande could hardly keep his feet, or his eyes open in the bitter spray. Then he was off his feet; he was hanging to the line, fighting out on it, calling to his foe, reaching for him. The brute must be swimming now, for the footing had gone from under them both.

Lalande felt a plunging on the line. It was too late now to hope to get the rope to the oak. The fighting horse was on it, and it began to give slowly past the man's hands. *La revanche* was bearing them on, the raft, the man, and the white devil who was its sole anchor, now. Lalande clung with one arm to the oak and drew in on the line. The dead weight of the raft had its way. The bucking, plunging brute, now touching the ground, now surging in the tide, was being drawn to him. Lalande began to call again. He had a great sense of pity for the stud. There were things that could not be withstood even by his lion heart; yet even the sea might not conquer except for this choking drag of the raft that held Rojas's grandchildren.

Lalande touched the stallion's muzzle now, coming on fighting with the obstinate ferocity of a white shark. He crouched in the crotch of the oak and held out his arms to the stallion's neck. When finally the brute crashed upon the sunken oak, Lalande reached his fingers to the cleft where the throw-rope cut into his neck. He dragged on the line, vainly trying to ease that tension. Once he thought of his knife; he might cut that choking grip from the white stud's throat. Then Lalande lay back in the crotch above the plunging hoofs and eased the great head above his own shoulder. Dragging on the line with all his power, he kept up his whispering as the hurricane tide rushed under them, swinging the oak on its roots, twisting it seaward, and sucking the earth away in whirls where Rojas's house had stood.

"I tell you we are still here, you and I," called Lalande after a while. "You and I, devil! You and I—smashed up together, my face against your own! *Eh, bien*! Be quiet, Émile Rojas may be watching his children, and you in this storm? Remember that, white devil, you have returned for them!" He laughed and shouted in the dark, his arm around the neck of the horse working his fingers under the rope, trying to take some of the strain upon his own flesh and bone. And presently he grumbled, "And remember, also, I am not a thief. Not a thief, eh?"

They clung that way five hours, until the crest of *la revanche* was passed. The sun even got through the huge rifts of black clouds streaming south by the time Old Rojas stirred about from his creaking raft in the scrub oaks. Everywhere a brown, dirty, sullen sea setting out, flecked with drift and wreckage, and of all Île Dautrive nothing showed but those few battered, branchless trees.

The stout old man waded waist-deep from his raft where now Émile's young ones sat up stiff and drowsy from the sea's nightlong flailing. He followed his mooring-line out to where it sogged under water by the big oak. The eldest boy had stood up looking after him.

"*Grand-père!*" screamed the lad suddenly. "Look! The white horse has come! By the tree, with the man!"

Old Rojas waded and struggled there, too astounded to speak. The sight was a queer one, indeed. The white horse was drawn against the oak crotch, pinned in there, in fact; and the rope from his neck also crushed the strange man against his shoulder. Joe Lalande appeared to be crucified against the satin coat of the stallion. But he lifted his free arm faintly when the old man floundered near them.

"M'sieu?" gasped Rojas. "You here?" He had to touch Lalande's drenched body ere he could believe that the man lived. Then he fell to loosening the slacked rope so that Lalande lurched down from the horse's neck into the water where he could hardly stand but clung to the tree trunk watching the animal. The rope had cut through Lalande's arm and shoulder until it made a long red-scarred mark from neck to elbow. He could not speak for a time with his salt-swollen lips.

"Yes, I am here," he whispered at last, and staggered weakly.

"Name of God, the white horse!" cried the old man. He put his hand out to touch the smooth side, but as if fearing him even now. Lalande was trying to discover whether or not the heart of the white stallion still beat; and then he turned away, his eyes closing wearily. He seemed to be shaken by a sob, a grief that the islander could not comprehend.

"What's the matter, M'sieu? We are safe; the boats will find us. *Le bon Dieu!* That was a storm! I have never seen a greater on this reef!"

Then he looked curiously at the still form of his old enemy. *"Eh, bien!* It took a white sea to kill this white devil, my friend!"

"It was not the sea," grumbled Lalande. "The touch of a rope on his neck, M'sieu. I saw his heart break last night, but it was for the children of Émile. A rope and the touch of my hand upon his neck, they were not to be endured, M'sieu." Then Lalande turned away, as it speaking to the lord of Dautrive against the tree: "At least you must know this, white devil, the hand on you was not the hand of a thief."

The Round-Up

[THEODORE ROOSEVELT]

During the wintertime there is ordinarily but little work done among the cattle. There is some line riding, and a continual lookout is kept for the very weak animals; but most of the stock are left to shift for themselves, undisturbed. Almost every stock-grower's association forbids branding any calves before the spring round-up. If great bands of cattle wander off the range, parties may be fitted out to go after them and bring them back; but this is only done when absolutely necessary, as when the drift of the cattle has been towards an Indian reservation or a settled granger country, for the weather is very severe, and the horses are so poor that their food must be carried along.

The bulk of the work is done during the summer, including the late spring and early fall, and consists mainly in a succession of round-ups, beginning, with us, in May and ending towards the last of October. But a good deal may be done by riding over one's range. Frequently, too, herding will be practiced on a large scale.

Still more important is the "trail" work; cattle, while driven from one range to another, or to a shipping point for beef, being said to be "on the trail." For years, the over-supply from the vast breeding ranches to the south, especially in Texas, has been driven northward in large herds, either to the shipping towns along the great railroads, or else to the fattening ranges of the Northwest; it having been found, so far, that while the calf crop is larger in the South, beeves become much heavier in the North. Such cattle, for the most part, went along tolerably well-marked routes or trails, which became for the time being of great importance, flourishing—and extremely lawless—towns growing up along them; but with the growth of the railroad system, and above all with the filling up of the northern ranges, these trails have steadily become of less and less consequence, though many herds still travel on them on their way to the already crowded ranges of western Dakota and Montana, or to the Canadian regions beyond. The trail work is something by itself. The herds may be on the trail several months, averaging fifteen miles or fewer a day. The cowboys accompanying each have to undergo much hard toil, of a peculiarly same and wearisome kind, on account of the extreme slowness with which everything must be done, as trail cattle should never be hurried. The foreman of a trail outfit must be not only a veteran cowhand, but also a miracle of patience and resolution.

Round-up work is far less irksome, there being an immense amount of dash and excitement connected with it; and when once the cattle are on the range, the important work is done during the round-up. On cow ranches, or wherever there is breeding stock, the spring round-up is the great event of the season, as it is then that the bulk of the calves are branded. It usually lasts six weeks, or thereabouts; but its end by no means implies rest for the stockman. On the contrary, as soon as it is over, wagons are sent to work out-of-the-way parts of the country that have been passed over, but where cattle are supposed to have drifted; and by the time these have come back the first beef round-up has begun, and thereafter beeves are steadily gathered and shipped, at least from among the larger herds, until cold weather sets in; and in the fall there is another round-up, to brand the late calves and see that the stock is got back on the range. As all of these round-ups are of one character, a description of the most important, taking place in the spring, will be enough.

In April we begin to get up the horses. Throughout the winter very few have been kept for use, as they are then poor and weak, and must be given grain and hay if they are to be worked. The men in the line camps need two or three apiece, and each man at the home ranch has a couple more; but the rest are left out to shift for themselves, which the tough, hardy little fellows are well able to do. Ponies can pick up a living where cattle die; though the scanty feed, which they may have to uncover by pawing off the snow, and the bitter weather often make them look very gaunt by springtime. But the first warm rains bring up the green grass, and then all the livestock gain flesh with wonderful rapidity. When the spring round-up begins the horses should be as fat and sleek as possible. After running all winter free, even the most sober pony is apt to betray an inclination to buck; and, if possible, we like to ride every animal once or twice before we begin to do real work with him. Animals that have escaped for any length of time are almost as bad to handle as if they had never been broken. One of the two horses mentioned in a preceding article as having been gone eighteen months has, since his return, been suggestively dubbed "Dynamite Jimmy," on account of the incessant and eruptive energy with which he bucks. Many of our horses, by the way, are thus named from some feat or peculiarity.

Wire Fence, when being broken, ran into one of the abominations after which he is now called; Hackamore once got away and remained out for three weeks with a hackamore, or breaking-halter, on him; Macaulay contracted the habit of regularly getting rid of the huge Scotchman to whom he was entrusted; Bulberry Johnny spent the hour or two after he was first mounted in a large patch of thorny bulberry bushes, his distracted rider unable to get him to do anything but move round sidewise in a circle; Fall Back would never get to the front; Water Skip always jumps mud puddles; and there are a dozen others with names as purely descriptive.

The stock-growers of Montana, of the western part of Dakota, and even of portions of extreme northern Wyoming—that is, of all the grazing lands lying in the basin of the Upper Missouri—have united and formed themselves into the great Montana Stock-Growers' Association. Among the countless benefits they have derived from this course, not the least has been the way in which the various round-ups work in with and supplement one another. At the spring meeting of the association, the entire territory mentioned above, including perhaps a hundred thousand square miles, is mapped out into round-up districts, which generally are changed but slightly from year to year, and the times and places for the round-ups to begin refixed so that those of adjacent districts may be run with a view to the best interests of all. Thus the stockmen along the Yellowstone have one round-up; we along the Little Missouri have another; and the country lying between, through which the Big Beaver flows, is almost equally important to both. Accordingly, one spring, the Little Missouri round-up, beginning May 25 and working downstream, was timed so as to reach the mouth of the Big Beaver about June 1, the Yellowstone round-up beginning at that date and place. Both then worked up the Beaver together to its head, when the Yellowstone men turned to the west and we bent back to our own river; thus the bulk of the strayed cattle of each were brought back to their respective ranges. Our own round-up district covers the Big and Little Beaver creeks, which rise near each other, but empty into the Little Missouri nearly a hundred and fifty miles apart, and so much of the latter river as lies between their mouths.

The captain or foreman of the round-up, upon whom very much of its efficiency and success depends, is chosen beforehand. He is, of course, an expert cowman, thoroughly acquainted with the country; and he must also be able to command and to keep control of the wild rough-riders he has under him—a feat needing both tact and firmness.

At the appointed day all meet at the place from which the round-up is to start. Each ranch, of course, has most work to be done in its own round-up district, but it is also necessary to have representatives in all those surrounding it. A large outfit may employ a dozen cowboys, or over, in the home district, and yet have nearly as many more representing its interest in the various ones adjoining. Smaller outfits generally club together to run a wagon and send outside representatives, or else go along with their stronger neighbors, their paying part of the expenses. A large outfit, with a herd of twenty thousand cattle or more, can, if necessary, run a round-up entirely by itself, and is able to act independently of outside help; it is therefore at a great advantage compared with those that can take no step effectively without their neighbor's consent and assistance.

If the starting point is some distance off, it may be necessary to leave home three or four days in advance. Before this we have got everything in readiness; have overhauled the wagons, shod any horse whose forefeet are tender—as a rule, all our ponies go barefooted—and left things in order at the ranch. Our outfit may be taken as a sample of everyone else's. We have a stout four-horse wagon to carry the bedding and the food; in its rear a mess-chest is rigged to hold the knives, forks, cans, etc. All our four team-horses are strong, willing animals, though of no great size, being originally just "broncos" or unbroken native horses, like the others. The teamster is also cook: a man who is a really first-rate hand at both driving and cooking—and our present teamster is both—can always command his price. Besides our own men, some cowboys from neighboring ranches and two or three representatives from other round-up districts are always along, and we generally have at least a dozen "riders," as they are termed—that is, cowboys, or "cowpunchers," who do the actual cattle work—with the wagon. Each of these has a string of eight or ten ponies; and to take charge of the saddle-band, thus consisting of a hundred-odd head, there are two herders, always known as "horse wranglers"—one for the day and one for the night. Occasionally there will be two wagons, one to carry the bedding and one the food, known, respectively, as the bed and the mess wagon; but this is not usual.

While traveling to the meeting point the pace is always slow, as it is an object to bring the horses on the ground as fresh as possible. Accordingly, we keep at a walk almost all day, and the riders, having nothing else to do, assist the wranglers in driving the saddle-band, three or four going in front, and others on the side, so that the horses shall keep on a walk. There is always some trouble with the animals at the starting out, as they are very fresh and are restive under the saddle. The herd is likely to stampede, and any beast that is frisky or vicious is sure to show its worst side. To do really effective cow-work a pony should be well broken; but many even of the old ones have vicious traits, and almost every man will have in his string one or two young horses, or broncos, hardly broken at all. In consequence, very many of my horses have to this day traits not calculated to set a timid or a clumsy rider at his ease. One or two run away and cannot be held by even the strongest bit; others can hardly be bridled or saddled until they have been thrown; two or three have a tendency to fall over backward; and half of them buck more or less, some so hard that only an expert can sit on them.

In riding these wild, vicious horses, and in careering over such very bad ground, especially at night, accidents are always occurring. A man who is merely an ordinary rider is certain to have a pretty hard time. On my first round-up I had a string of nine horses, four of them broncos, only broken to the extent of having each been saddled once or twice. One of them it was an impossibility to bridle or to saddle single-handed; it was very difficult to get on or off him, and he was exceedingly nervous if a man moved his hands or feet; but he had no bad tricks. The second soon became perfectly quiet. The third turned out to be one of the worst buckers on the ranch; once, when he bucked me off, I managed to fall on a stone and broke a rib. The fourth had a still worse habit, for he would balk and then throw himself over backward; once, when I was not quick enough, he caught me and broke something in the point of my shoulder, so that it was some weeks before I could raise the arm freely. My hurts were far from serious, and did not interfere with my riding and working as usual through the round-up; but I was heartily glad when it ended, and ever since have religiously done my best to get none but gentle horses in my own string. However, everyone gets falls from or with his horse now and then in cow country; and even my men, good riders though they are, are sometimes injured. One of them once broke his ankle; another a rib; another was on one occasion stunned, remaining unconscious for some hours; and yet another had certain of his horses buck under him so hard and long as finally to hurt his lungs and make him cough blood. Fatal accidents occur annually in almost every district, especially if there is much work to be done among stampeded cattle at night; but on my own ranch none of my men has ever been seriously hurt, though on one occasion a cowboy from another ranch, who was with my wagon, was killed, his horse falling and pitching him heavily on his head.

For bedding, each man has two or three pairs of blankets, and a tarpaulin or small wagon-sheet. Usually, two or three sleep together. Even in June the nights are generally cool and pleasant, and it is chilly in the early mornings; although this is not always so, and when the weather stays hot and mosquitoes are plenty, the hours of darkness, even in midsummer, seem painfully long. In the Bad Lands proper we are not often bothered very seriously by these winged pests; but in the low bottoms of the Big Missouri, and beside many of the reedy ponds and great sloughs out on the prairie, they are a perfect scourge. During the very hot nights, when they are especially active, the bedclothes make a man feel absolutely smothered, and yet his only chance for sleep is to wrap himself tightly up, head and all, and even then some of the pests will usually force their way in. At sunset I have seen the mosquitoes rise up from the land like a dense cloud, to make the hot, stifling night one long torture; the horses would neither lie down nor graze, traveling restlessly to and fro till daybreak, their bodies streaked and bloody, and the insects settling on them so as to make them all one color, a uniform gray; while the men, after a few hours' tossing about in the vain attempt to sleep, rose, built a little fire of damp sagebrush, and thus endured the misery as best they could until it was light enough to work.

But if the weather is fine, a man will never sleep better nor more pleasantly than in the open air after a hard day's work on the round-up; nor will an ordinary shower or gust of wind disturb him in the least, for he simply draws the tarpaulin over his head and goes on sleeping. But now and then we have a windstorm that might better be called a whirlwind and has to be met very differently; and two or three days or nights of rain ensure the wetting of the blankets, and therefore shivering discomfort on the part of the would-be sleeper. For two or three hours all goes well; and it is rather soothing to listen to the steady patter of the great raindrops on the canvas. But then it will be found that a corner has been left open through which the water can get in, or else the tarpaulin will begin to leak somewhere; or perhaps the water will have collected in a hollow underneath and have begun to soak through. Soon a little stream trickles in, and every effort to remedy matters merely results in a change for the worse. To move out of the way ensures getting wet in a fresh spot; and the best course is to lie still and accept the evils that have come with what fortitude one can. Even thus, the first night a man can sleep pretty well; but if the rain continues, the second night, when the blankets are already damp, and when the water comes through more easily, is apt to be the most unpleasant.

Of course, a man can take little spare clothing on a round-up; at the very outside two or three clean handkerchiefs, a pair of socks, a change of underclothes, and the most primitive kind of washing apparatus, all wrapped up in a stout jacket which is to be worn when night-herding. The inevitable "slicker," or oilskin coat, which gives complete protection from the wet, is always carried behind the saddle.

At the meeting place there is usually a delay of a day or two to let everyone come in; and the plain on which the encampment is made becomes a scene of great bustle and turmoil. The heavy four-horse wagons jolt in from different quarters, the horse wranglers rushing madly to and fro in the endeavor to keep the different saddle-bands from mingling, while the "riders," or cowboys, with each wagon jog along in a body. The representatives from outside districts ride in singly or by twos and threes, every man driving before him his own horses, one of them loaded with his bedding. Each wagon wheels out of the way into some camping place not too near the others, the bedding is tossed out on the ground, and then everyone is left to do what he wishes, while the different wagon bosses, or foremen, seek out the captain of the round-up to learn what his plans are.

There is a good deal of rough but effective discipline and method in the way in which a round-up is carried on. The captain of the whole has as lieutenants the various wagon foremen, and in making demands for men to do some special service he will usually merely designate some foreman to take charge of the work and let him parcel it out among his men to suit himself. The captain of the round-up or the foreman of a wagon may himself be a ranchman; if such is not the case, and the ranchman nevertheless comes along, he works and fares precisely as do the other cowboys.

While the head men are gathered in a little knot, planning out the work, the others are dispersed over the plain in every direction, racing, breaking rough horses, or simply larking with one another. If a man has an especially bad horse, he usually takes such an opportunity, when he has plenty of time, to ride him; and while saddled he is surrounded by a crowd of most unsympathetic associates who greet with uproarious mirth any misadventure. A man on a bucking horse is always considered fair game, every squeal and jump of the bronco being hailed with cheers of delighted irony for the rider and shouts to "stay with him." The antics of a vicious bronco show infinite variety of detail, but are all modeled on one general plan. When the rope settles round his neck the fight begins, and it is only after much plunging and snorting that a twist is taken over his nose, or else a hackamore—a species of severe halter, usually made of plaited hair—slipped on his head. While being bridled he strikes viciously with his forefeet, and perhaps has to be blindfolded or thrown down; and to get the saddle on him is quite as difficult. When saddled, he may get rid of his exuberant spirits by bucking under the saddle, or may reserve all his energies for the rider. In the latter case, the man, keeping tight hold with his left hand of the cheek-strap, so as to prevent the horse from getting his head down until he is fairly seated, swings himself quickly into the saddle. Up rises the bronco's back into an arch; his head, the ears laid straight back, goes down between his forefeet, and, squealing savagely, he makes a succession of rapid, stiff-legged, jarring bounds. Sometimes he is a "plunging" bucker, who runs forward all the time while bucking; or he may buck steadily in one place, or "sunfish"—that is, bring first one shoulder down almost to the ground and then the other—or else he may change ends while in the air. A first-class rider will sit throughout it all without moving from the saddle, quirting (Spanish term for a short flexible riding whip used throughout cowboy land) his horse all the time, though his hat may be jarred off his head and his revolver out of its sheath. After a few jumps, however, the average man grasps hold of the horn of the saddle—the delighted onlookers meanwhile earnestly advising him not to "go to leather"—and is contented to get through the affair in any shape, provided he can escape without being thrown off. An accident is of necessity borne with a broad grin, as any attempt to resent the raillery of the bystanders—which is perfectly good-humored—would be apt to result disastrously. Cowboys are certainly extremely good riders. As a class they have no superiors. Of course, they would at first be at a disadvantage in steeple-chasing or fox-hunting, but their average of horsemanship is without doubt higher than that of the men who take part in these latter amusements. A cowboy would learn to ride across the country in a quarter of the time it would take a cross-country rider to learn to handle a vicious bronco or to do good cow-work round and in a herd.

On such a day, when there is no regular work, there will often be horse races, as each outfit is pretty sure to have some running pony which it believes can outpace any other. These contests are always short-distance dashes, for but a few hundred yards. Horse racing is a mania with most plainsmen, white or red. A man with a good racing pony will travel all about with it, often winning large sums, visiting alike cow ranches, frontier towns, and Indian encampments. Sometimes the race is "pony against pony," the victor taking both steeds. In racing, the men ride bareback, as there are hardly any light saddles in the cow country. There will be intense excitement and very heavy betting over a race between two well-known horses, together with a good chance of blood being shed in the attendant quarrels. Indians and whites often race against each other as well as among themselves. I have seen several such contests, and in every case but one the white man happened to win. A race is usually run between two thick rows of spectators, on foot and on horseback, and as the racers pass, these rows close in behind them, every man yelling and shouting with all the strength of his lungs, and all waving their hats and cloaks to encourage the contestants, or firing off their revolvers and saddle guns. The little horses are fairly maddened, as is natural enough, and run as if they were crazy: were the distances any longer, some would be sure to drop in their tracks.

Besides the horse races, which are, of course, the main attraction, the men at a round-up will often get up wrestling matches or foot races. In fact, everyone feels that he is off for a holiday; for after the monotony of a long winter, the cowboys look forward eagerly to the round-up, where the work is hard, it is true, but exciting and varied, and treated a good deal as a frolic. There is no eight-hour law in cowboy land; during round-up time we often count ourselves lucky if we get off with much fewer than sixteen hours; but the work is done in the saddle, and the men are spurred on all the time by the desire to outdo one another in feats of daring and skillful horsemanship. There is very little quarreling or fighting, and though the fun often takes the form of rather rough horseplay, yet the practice of carrying dangerous weapons makes cowboys show far more rough courtesy to each other and far less rudeness to strangers than is the case among, for instance, Eastern miners, or even lumbermen. When a quarrel may very probably result fatally, a man thinks twice before going into it; warlike people or classes always treat one another with a certain amount of consideration and politeness. The moral tone of a cow camp, indeed, is rather high than otherwise. Meanness, cowardice, and dishonesty are not tolerated. There is a high regard for truthfulness and keeping one's word, intense contempt for any kind of hypocrisy, and a hearty dislike for a man who shirks his work. Many of the men gamble and drink, but many do neither; and the conversation is not worse than in most bodies composed wholly of male human beings. A cowboy will not submit tamely to an insult, and is very ready to avenge his own wrongs; nor has he an overwrought fear of shedding blood. He possesses, in fact, few of the emasculated, milk-and-water moralities admired by the pseudo-philanthropists; but he does possess, to a very high degree, the stern, manly qualities that are so valuable to a nation.

The method of work is simple. The mess-wagons and loose horses, after breaking camp in the morning, move on in a straight line for some few miles, going into camp again before midday; and the day herd, consisting of all the cattle that have been found far off their range, and which are to be brought back there, and of any others that it is necessary to gather, follows on afterwards. Meanwhile, the cowboys scatter out and drive in all the cattle from the country round about, going perhaps ten or fifteen miles back from the line of march, and meeting at the place where camp has already been pitched. The wagons always keep some little distance from one another, and the saddle-bands do the same, so that the horses may not get mixed. It is rather picturesque to see the four-horse teams filing down at a trot through a pass among the buttes—the saddle-bands being driven along at a smart place to one side or behind, the teamsters cracking their whips, and the horse wranglers calling and shouting as they ride rapidly from side to side behind the horses, urging on the stragglers by dexterous touches with the knotted ends of their long lariats that are left trailing from the saddle. The country driven over is very rough, and it is often necessary to double up teams and put on eight horses to each wagon in going up an unusually steep pitch, or hauling through a deep mud-hole, or over a river crossing where there is quicksand.

The speed and thoroughness with which a country can be worked depends, of course, very largely upon the number of riders. Ours is probably about an average round-up as regards size. The last spring I was out, there were half a dozen wagons along; the saddle-bands numbered about a hundred each; and the morning we started, sixty men in the saddle splashed along the shallow ford of the river that divided the plain where we had camped from the valley of the long winding creek up which we were first to work.

In the morning, the cook is preparing breakfast long before the first glimmer of dawn. As soon as it is ready, probably about 3 o'clock, he utters a long-drawn shout, and all the sleepers feel it is time to be up on the instant, for they know there can be no such thing as delay on the round-up, under penalty of being set afoot. Accordingly, they bundle out, rubbing their eyes and yawning, draw on their boots and trousers—if they have taken the latter off—roll up and cord their bedding, and usually without any attempt at washing crowd over to the little smoldering fire, which is placed in a hole dug in the ground, so that there may be no risk of its spreading. The men are rarely very hungry at breakfast, and it is a meal that has to be eaten in shortest order, so it is perhaps the least important. Each man, as he comes up, grasps a tin cup and plate from the mess-box, pours out his tea or coffee, with sugar, but of course no milk, helps himself to one or two of the biscuits that have been baked in a Dutch oven, and perhaps also to a slice of the fat pork swimming in the grease of the frying pan, ladles himself out some beans, if there are any, and squats down on the ground to eat his breakfast. The meal is not an elaborate one; nevertheless a man will have to hurry if he wishes to eat it before hearing the foreman sing out, "Come, boys, catch your horses;" when he must drop everything and run out to the wagon with his lariat. The night wrangler is now bringing in the saddle-band, which he has been up all night guarding. A rope corral is rigged up by stretching a rope from each wheel of one side of the wagon, making a V-shaped space, into which the saddle horses are driven. Certain men stand around to keep them inside, while the others catch the horses; many outfits have one man do all the roping, As soon as each has caught his horse—usually a strong, tough animal, the small, quick ponies being reserved for the work round the herd in the afternoon—the band, now in charge of the day wrangler, is turned loose, and everyone saddles up as fast as possible. It still lacks some time of being sunrise, and the air has in it the peculiar chill of the early morning. When all are saddled, many of the horses bucking and dancing about, the riders from the different wagons all assemble at the one where the captain is sitting, already mounted. He waits a very short time—for laggards receive but scant mercy—before announcing the proposed camping place and parceling out the work among those present. If, as is usually the case, the line of march is along a river or creek, he appoints some man to take a dozen others and drive down (or up) it ahead of the day herd, so that the latter will not have to travel through other cattle; the day herd itself being driven and guarded by a dozen men detached for that purpose. The rest of the riders are divided into two bands, placed under men who know the country, and start out, one on each side, to bring in every head for fifteen miles back. The captain then himself rides down to the new camping place, so as to be there as soon as any cattle are brought in.

Meanwhile, the two bands, a score of riders in each, separate and make their way in opposite directions. The leader of each tries to get such a "scatter" on his men that they will cover completely all the land gone over. This morning work is called circle riding, and is peculiarly hard in the Bad Lands on account of the remarkably broken, rugged nature of the country. The men come in on lines that tend to a common center—as if the sticks of a fan were curved. As the band goes out, the leader from time to time detaches one or two men to ride down through certain sections of the country, making the shorter, or what are called inside, circles, while he keeps on; and finally, retaining as companions the two or three whose horses are toughest, makes the longest or outside circle himself, going clear back to the divide, or whatever the point may be that marks the limit of the round-up work, and then turning and working straight to the meeting place. Each man, of course, brings in every head of cattle he can see.

These long, swift rides in the glorious spring mornings are not soon to be forgotten. The sweet, fresh air with a touch of sharpness thus early in the day, and the rapid motion of the fiery little horse combine to make a man's blood thrill and leap with sheer buoyant light-heartedness and eager, exultant pleasure in the boldness and freedom of the life he is leading. As we climb the steep sides of the first range of buttes, wisps of wavering mist still cling in the hollows of the valley; when we come out on the top of the first great plateau, the sun flames up over its edge, and in the level, red beams the galloping horsemen throw long, fantastic shadows. Black care rarely sits behind a rider whose pace is fast enough; at any rate, not when he first feels the horse move under him.

Sometimes we trot or pace, and again we lope or gallop; the few who are to take the outside circle must needs ride both hard and fast. Although only grass-fed, the horses are tough and wiry; and more-

over, are each used but once in four days or thereabouts, so they stand the work well. The course out
lies across great grassy plateaus, among knife-like
ridge crests, among winding valleys and ravines, and
over acres of barren, sun-scorched buttes that look
grimly grotesque and forbidding, while in the Bad
Lands the riders unhesitatingly go down and over
places where it seems impossible that a horse should
even stand. The line of horsemen will quarter down
the site of a butte, where every pony has to drop
from ledge to ledge like a goat, and will go over the
shoulder of the soapstone cliff, when wet and slippery, with a series of plunges and scrambles which,
if unsuccessful, would land horses and riders in the
bottom of the canyon-like washout below. In de-
scending a clay butte after a rain, the pony will put
all four feet together and side down to the bottom
almost or quite on his haunches. In very wet
weather the Bad Lands are absolutely impassable;
but if the ground is not slippery, it is a remarkable
place that can shake the matter-of-course confidence felt by the rider in the capacity of his steed to
go anywhere.

Esmé

[SAKI (H.H. MUNRO)]

" 'Unting is the sport of kings, the image of war without its guilt and only five and twenty percent of its danger!"—Jorrocks

"All hunting stories are the same, " said Clovis; "just as all Turf stories are the same, and all—"

"My hunting story isn't a bit like any you've ever heard," said the Baroness. "It happened quite a while ago, when I was about twenty-three. I wasn't living apart from my husband then; you see, neither of us could afford to make the other a separate allowance. In spite of everything that proverbs may say, poverty keeps together more homes than it breaks up. But we always hunted with different packs. All this has nothing to do with the story."

"We haven't arrived at the meet yet. I suppose there was a meet," said Clovis.

"Of course there was a meet," said the Baroness; "all the usual crowd were there, especially Constance Broddle. Constance is one of those strapping florid girls that goes so well with autumn scenery or Christmas decorations in church. 'I feel a presentiment that something dreadful is going to happen,' she said to me. 'Am I looking pale?'

"She was looking about as pale as a beet root that has suddenly heard bad news.

"'You're looking nicer than usual,' I said, 'but that's so easy for you.' Before she had got the right bearings of this remark we had settled down to business; hounds had found a fox lying out in some gorse bushes."

"I knew it," said Clovis. "In every foxhunting story that I've ever heard there's been a fox and some gorse bushes."

"Constance and I were well mounted," continued the Baroness serenely, "and we had no difficulty in keeping ourselves in the first flight, though it was a fairly stiff run. Towards the finish, however, we must have held rather too independent a line, for we lost the hounds, and found ourselves plodding aimlessly along miles away from anywhere. It was fairly exasperating, and my temper was beginning to let itself go by inches, when on pushing our way

through an accommodating hedge, we were glad-
dened by the sight of hounds in full cry in a hollow just beneath us.

"'There they go,' cried Constance, and then added
in a gasp, 'In Heaven's name, what are they hunting?'

"It was certainly no mortal fox. It stood more
than twice as high, had a short, ugly head, and an
enormous thick neck.

"'It's a hyaena,' I cried; 'it must have escaped from
Lord Pabham's Park.'

"At that moment the hunted beast turned and
faced its pursuers, and the hounds (there were only
about six couple then) stood round in a half-circle
and looked foolish. Evidently they had broken away
from the rest of the pack on the trail of this alien
scent, and were not quite sure how to treat the
quarry now they had got him.

"The hyaena hailed our approach with unmistak-
able relief and demonstrations of friendliness. It had
probably been accustomed to uniform kindness
from humans, while its first experience of a pack of
hounds had left a bad impression. The hounds
looked more than ever embarrassed as their quarry
paraded its sudden intimacy with us, and the faint
toot of a horn in the distance was seized on as a
welcome signal for unobtrusive departure. Constance and I and the hyaena were left alone in the
gathering twilight.

"'What are we to do?' asked Constance.

"'What a person you are for questions,' I said.

"'Well, we can't stay here all night with a hyaena,' she retorted.

"'I don't know what your ideas of comfort are,' I said; "but I shouldn't think of staying here all night even without a hyaena. My home may be an unhappy one, but at least it has hot and cold water laid on, and domestic service, and other conveniences which we shouldn't find here. We had better make for that ridge of trees to the right; I imagine the Crowley road is just beyond.'

"We trotted off slowly along a faintly marked cart track, with the beast following cheerfully at our heels.

"'What on earth are we to do with the hyaena?' came the inevitable question.

"'What does one generally do with hyaenas?' I asked crossly.

"'I've never had anything to do with one before,' said Constance.

"'Well, neither have I. If we even knew its sex we might give it a name. Perhaps we might call it Esmé. That would do in either case.'

"There was still sufficient daylight for us to distinguish wayside objects, and our listless spirits gave an upward perk as we came upon a small half-naked gypsy brat picking blackberries from a low-growing bush. The sudden apparition of two horsewomen and a hyaena set it off crying, and in any case we should have scarcely gleaned any useful geographical information from that source; but there was a probability that we might strike a gypsy encampment somewhere along our route. We rode on hopefully but uneventfully for another mile or so.

"'I wonder what that child was doing there,' said Constance presently.

"'Picking blackberries, obviously.'

"'I don't like the way it cried,' pursued Constance; 'somehow its wail keeps ringing in my ears.'

"I did not chide Constance for her morbid fancies; as a matter of face the same sensation, of being pursued by a persistent fretful wail, had been forcing itself on my rather overtired nerves. For company's sake I hulloed to Esmé, who had lagged somewhat behind. With a few springy bounds he drew up level, and then shot past us.

"The wailing accompaniment was explained. The gypsy child was firmly, and I expect painfully, held in his jaws.

"'Merciful Heaven!' screamed Constance, 'what on earth shall we do? What are we to do?'

"I am perfectly certain that at the Last Judgment Constance will ask more questions than any of the examining Seraphs.

"'Can't we do something?' she persisted tearfully, as Esmé cantered along easily in front of our tired horses.

"Personally I was doing everything that occurred to me at the moment. I stormed and scolded and coaxed in English and French and gamekeeper language; I made absurd, ineffectual cuts in the air with my thongless hunting crop; I hurled my sandwich case at the brute; in fact, I really don't know what more I could have done. And still we lumbered on through the deepening dusk, with the dark uncouth shape lumbering ahead of us, and a drone of lugubrious music floating in our ears. Suddenly Esmé bounded aside into some thick bushes, where we could not follow; the wail rose to a shriek and then stopped altogether. This part of the story I always hurry over, because it is really rather horrible. When the beast joined us again, after an absence of a few minutes, there was an air of patient understanding about him, as though he knew that he had done something of which we disapproved, but which he felt to be thoroughly justifiable.

"'How can you let that ravening beast trot by your side?' asked Constance. She was looking more than ever like an albino beet root.

"'In the first place, I can't prevent it,' I said, 'and in the second place, whatever else he may be, I doubt if he's ravening at the present moment.'

"Constance shuddered. 'Do you think the poor little thing suffered much?' came another of her futile questions.

"'The indications were all that way,' I said. 'On the other hand, of course, it may have been crying from sheer temper. Children sometimes do.'

"It was nearly pitch-dark when we emerged suddenly into the high road. A flash of lights and the whir of a motor went past us at the same moment at uncomfortably close quarters. A thud and a sharp screeching yowl followed a second later. The car drew up, and when I had ridden back to the spot I found a young man bending over a dark motionless mass lying by the roadside.

"'You have killed my Esmé,' I exclaimed bitterly.

"'I'm so awfully sorry,' said the young man; 'I keep dogs myself, so I know what you must feel about it. I'll do anything I can in reparation.'

"'Please bury him at once,' I said; 'that much I think I may ask of you.'

"'Bring the spade, William,' he called to the chauffeur. Evidently hasty roadside interments were contingencies that had been provided against.

"The digging of a sufficiently large grave took some time. 'I say, what a magnificent fellow,' said the motorist as the corpse was rolled over into the trench. 'I'm afraid he must have been rather a valuable animal.'

"'He took second in the puppy class at Birmingham last year,' I said resolutely.

"Constance snorted loudly.

"'Don't cry, dear,' I said brokenly; 'it was all over in a moment. He couldn't have suffered much.'

"'Look here,' said the young fellow desperately, 'you simply must let me do something by way of reparation.'

"I refused sweetly, but as he persisted I let him have my address.

"Of course, we kept our own counsel as to the earlier episodes of the evening. Lord Pabham never advertised the loss of his hyaena; when a strictly fruit-eating animal strayed from his park a year or two previously he was called upon to give compensation in eleven cases of sheep-worrying and practically to restock his neighbor's poultry yards, and an escaped hyaena would have mounted up to the something on the scale of a government grant. The gypsies were equally unobtrusive over their missing offspring; I don't suppose in large encampments they really know to a child or two how many they've got."

The Baroness paused reflectively, and then continued:

"There was a sequel to the adventure, though. I got through the post a charming little diamond brooch, with the name Esmé set in a sprig of rosemary. Incidentally, too, I lost the friendship of Constance Broddle. You see, when I sold the brooch I quite properly refused to give her any share of the proceeds. I pointed out that the Esmé part of the affair was my own invention, and the hyaena part of it belonged to Lord Pabham, if it really was his hyaena, of which, of course, I've no proof."

The Geebung Polo Club

[A.B. "BANJO" PATERSON]

It was somewhere up the country in a land of
rock and scrub,
That they formed an institution called the
Geebung Polo Club.
They were long and wiry natives of the rugged
mountainside,
And the horse was never saddled that the Geebungs
couldn't ride;
But their style of playing polo was irregular and
rash—
They had mighty little science, but a mighty lot of
dash:
And they played on mountain ponies that were
muscular and strong,
Though their coats were quite unpolished, and their
manes and tails were long.

And they used to train those ponies wheeling cattle
   in the scrub;
They were demons, were the members of the Geebung Polo Club.

It was somewhere down the country, in a city's
   smoke and steam,
That a polo club existed, called the Cuff and Collar
   Team.
As a social institution 'twas a marvelous success,
For the members were distinguished by exclusive-
   ness and dress.
They had natty little ponies that were nice, and
   smooth, and sleek,
For their cultivated owners only rode 'em once a
   week.
So they started up the country in pursuit of sport
   and fame,
For they meant to show the Geebungs how they
   ought to play the game;
And they took their valets with them—just to give
   their boots a rub
Ere they started operations on the Geebung Polo
   Club.

Now my readers can imagine how the contest
   ebbed and flowed,

When the Geebung boys got going it was time to
    clear the road;
And the game was so terrific that ere half the time
    was gone
A spectator's leg was broken—just from merely
    looking on.
For they waddied one another till the plain was
    strewn with dead,
While the score was kept so even that they neither
    got ahead.
And the Cuff and Collar captain, when he tumbled
    off to die,
Was the last surviving player—so the game was
    called a tie.

Then the captain of the Geebungs raised him slowly
    from the ground,
Though his wounds were mostly mortal, yet he
    fiercely gazed around;
There was no one to oppose him—all the rest were
    in a trance,
So he scrambled on his pony for his last expiring
    chance,
For he meant to make an effort to get victory to his
    side;
So he struck at goal—and missed it—and he
    tumbled off and died.

By the old Campaspe River, where the breezes
  shake the grass,
There's a row of little gravestones that the stockmen
  never pass,
For they bear a crude inscription saying, "Stranger,
  drop a tear,
For the Cuff and Collar players and the Geebung
  boys lie here."
And on misty moonlit evenings, while the dingoes
  howl around,
You can see their shadows flitting down that phan-
  tom polo ground;
You can hear the loud collisions as the flying play-
  ers meet,
And the rattle of the mallets, and the rush of ponies'
  feet,
Till the terrified spectator rides like blazes to the
  pub-
He's been haunted by the specters of the Geebung
  Polo Club.

Roughing It

[MARK TWAIN]

In a little while all interest was taken up in stretching our necks and watching for the "pony-rider"—the fleet messenger who sped across the continent from St. Joe to Sacramento, carrying letters nineteen hundred miles in eight days! Think of that for perishable horse and human flesh and blood to do! The pony-rider was usually a little bit of a man, brimful of spirit and endurance. No matter what time of the day or night his watch came on, and no matter whether it was winter or summer, raining, snowing, hailing, or sleeting, or whether his "beat" was a level straight road or a crazy trail over mountain crags and precipices, or whether it lead through peaceful regions or regions that swarmed with hostile Indians, he must be always ready to leap into the saddle and be off like the wind!

There was no idling-time for a pony-rider on duty. He rode fifty miles without stopping, by daylight, moonlight, starlight, or through the blackness of darkness—just as it happened. He rode a splendid horse that was born for a racer and fed and lodged like a gentleman; kept him at his utmost speed for ten miles, and then, as he came crashing up to the station where stood two men holding fast a fresh, impatient steed, the transfer of rider and mail-bag was made in the twinkling of an eye, and away flew the eager pair and were out of sight before the spectator could get hardly the ghost of a look.

Both rider and horse went "flying light." The rider's dress was thin, and fitted close; he wore a "round-about," and a skull-cap, and tucked his pantaloons into his boot-tops like a race-rider. He carried no arms—he carried nothing that was not absolutely necessary, for even the postage on his literary freight was worth five dollars a letter.

"HERE HE COMES"

He got but little frivolous correspondence to carry—his bag had business letters in it, mostly. His horse was stripped of all unnecessary weight, too. He wore a little wafer of a racing-saddle, and no visible blanket. He wore light shoes, or none at all. The little flat mail-pockets strapped under the rider's thighs would each hold about the bulk of a child's primer. They held many and many an important business chapter and newspaper letter, but these were written on paper as airy and thin as gold leaf, nearly, and thus bulk and weight were economized. The stagecoach traveled about a hundred to a hundred and twenty-five miles a day (twenty-four hours), the pony-rider about two hundred and fifty. There were about eighty pony-riders in the saddle all the time, night and day, stretching in a long, scattering procession from Missouri to California, forty flying eastward, and forty towards the west, and among them making four hundred gallant horses earn a stirring livelihood and see a deal of scenery every single day in the year.

We had had a consuming desire, from the beginning, to see a pony-rider, but somehow or other all that passed us and all that met us managed to streak by in the night, and so we heard only a whiz and a hail, and the swift phantom of the desert was gone before we could get our heads out of the windows. But now we were expecting one along every moment, and would see him in broad daylight. Presently the driver exclaims: "HERE HE COMES!"

Every neck is stretched further, and every eye strained wider. Away across the endless dead level of the prairie a black speck appears against the sky, and it is plain that it moves. Well, I should think so!

CHANGING HORSES

In a second or two it becomes a horse and rider, rising and falling, rising and falling—sweeping towards us nearer and nearer—growing more and more distinct, more and more sharply defined— nearer and still nearer, and the flutter of the hoofs comes faintly to the ear—another instant a whoop and a hurrah from our upper deck, a wave of the rider's hand, but no reply, and man and horse burst past our excited faces, and go winging away like a belated fragment of a storm!

So sudden is it all, and so like a flash of unreal fancy, that but for the flake of white foam left quivering and perishing on a mail-sack after the vision had flashed by and disappeared, we might have doubted whether we had seen any actual horse and man at all, maybe.

"The Man Who Hunts and Doesn't Like It" from Hunting Sketches

[**ANTHONY TROLLOPE**]

It seems to be odd, at first sight, that there should be any such men as these; but their name and number are legion. If we were to deduct from the hunting-crowd farmers, and others who hunt because hunting is brought to their door, of the remainder we should find that the "men who don't like it" have the preponderance. It is pretty much the same, I think, with all amusements. How many men go to balls, to races, to the theatre, how many women to concerts and races, simply because it is the thing to do? They have, perhaps, a vague idea that they may ultimately find some joy in the pastime; but, though they do the thing constantly, they never like it. Of all such men, the hunting men are perhaps the most to be pitied.

They are easily recognized by anyone who cares to scrutinize the men around him in the hunting field. It is not to be supposed that all those who, in common parlance, do not ride, are to be included among the number of hunting men who don't like it. Many a man who sticks constantly to the roads and lines of gates—who, from principle, never looks at a fence, is much attached to hunting. Some of those who have borne great names as Nimrods in our hunting annals would as life have led a forlorn hope as put a horse at a flight of hurdles. But they, too, are known; and though the nature of their delight is a mystery to straight-going men, it is manifest enough that they do like it. Their theory of hunting is at any rate plain. They have an acknowledged system, and know what they are doing. But the men who don't like it, have no system, and never know distinctly what is their own aim. During some portion of their career they commonly try to ride hard, and sometimes for a while they will succeed. In short spurts, while the cherry brandy prevails, they often have small successes; but even with the assistance of a spur in the head they never like it.

Dear old John Leech! What an eye he had for the man who hunts and doesn't like it! But for such, as a pictorial chronicler of the hunting field he would have had no fame. Briggs, I fancy, in his way did like it. Briggs was a full-blooded, up-apt, awkward, san-guine man, who was able to like anything, from gin and water upwards. But with how many a wretched companion of Briggs's are we not familiar? Men as to whom any girl of eighteen would swear from the form of his visage and the carriage of his legs as he sits on his horse that he was seeking honour where honour was not to be found, and looking for pleas-ure in places where no pleasure lay for him.

But the man who hunts and doesn't like it has his moments of gratification, and finds a source of pride in his penance. In the summer, hunting does much for him. He does not usually take much personal care of his horses, as he is probably a town man and his horses are summered by a keeper of hunting sta-bles; but he talks of them. He talks of them freely, and the keeper of the hunting stables is occasionally forced to write to him. And he can run down to look at his nags, and spend a few hours eating bad mutton chops, walking about the yards and pad-docks, and, bleeding half crowns through the nose. In all this there is a delight which offers some com-pensation for his winter misery to our friend who hunts and doesn't like it.

He finds it pleasant to talk of his horses especially to young women, with whom, perhaps, the ascer-tained fact of his winter employment does give him some credit. It is still something to be a hunting man even yet, though the multiplicity of railways and the existing plethora of money has so increased the number of sportsmen, that to keep a nag or two near some well-known station, is nearly as common as to die. But the delight of these martyrs is at the highest in the presence of their tailors; or, higher still, perhaps, in that of their bootmakers. The hunting man does receive some honour from him who makes his breeches; and, with a well-balanced sense of justice, the tailor's foreman is, I think, more patient, more admiring, more demonstrative in his assurances, more ready with his bit of chalk, when handling the knee of the man who doesn't like the work, than he ever is with the customer who comes to him simply because he wants some clothes fit for the saddle. The judicious conciliating tradesman knows that compensation should be given, and he helps to give it. But the visits to the bootmaker are better still. The tailor persists in telling his customer how his breeches should be made, and after what fashion they should be worn, but the bootmaker will take his orders meekly. If not ruffled by paltry objections as to the fit of the foot, he will accede to any amount of instructions as to the legs and tops. And then a new pair of top boots is a pretty toy; costly, perhaps, if needed only as a toy, but very pretty, and more decorative in a gentleman's dressing room than any other type of garment. And top boots, when multiplied in such a locality—when seen in a phalanx—tell such pleasant lies on their owner's behalf. While your breeches are as dumb in their retirement as though you had not paid for them, your conspicuous boots are eloquent with a thousand tongues! There is pleasure found, no doubt, in this.

As the season draws nigh the delights become vague, and still more vague; but, nevertheless, there are delights. Getting up at six o'clock in November to go down to Bletchley by an early train is not in itself pleasant, but on the opening morning—on the few first opening mornings—there is a promise about the thing which invigorates and encourages the early riser. He means to like it this year—if he can. He has still some undefined notion that his period of pleasure will now come. He has not, as yet, accepted the adverse verdict which his own nature has given against him in this matter of hunting, and he gets into his early tub with acme glow of satisfaction. And afterwards it is nice to find himself bright with mahogany tops, buff-tinted breeches, and a pink coat. The ordinary habiliments of an English gentleman are so somber that his own eye is gratified, and he feels that he has placed himself in the vanguard of society by thus shining in his apparel. And he will ride this year! He is fixed to that purpose. He will ride straight—and, if possible, he will like it.

But the Ethiop cannot change his skin, nor can any man add a cubit to his stature. He doesn't like it, and all around him in the field know how it is with him. He himself knows how it is with others like himself, and he congregates with his brethren. The period of his penance has come upon him. He has to pay the price of those pleasant interviews with his tradesmen. He has to expiate the false boasts made to his female cousins. That row of boots cannot be made to shine in his chamber for nothing. The hounds have found, and the fox is away. Men are fastening on their flat-topped hats and feeling themselves in their stirrups. Horses are hot for the run, and the moment for liking it has come—if only it were possible!

But at moments such as these something has to be done. The man who doesn't like it, let him dislike it ever so much, Cannot check his horse and simply ride back to the hunting stables. He understands that were he to do that, he must throw up his cap at once and resign. Nor can he trot easily along the roads with the fat old country gentleman who is out on his rough cob, and who, looking up to the wind and remembering the position of adjacent coverts, will give a good guess as to the direction in which the field will move. No, he must make an effort. The time of his penance has come, and the penance must be borne. There is a spark of pluck about him, though unfortunately he has brought it to bear in a wrong direction. The blood still runs at his heart, and he resolves that he will ride—if only he could tell which way.

The stout gentleman on the cob has taken the road to the left with a few companions, but our friend knows that the stout gentleman has a little game of his own which will not be suitable for one who intends to ride. Then the crowd in front has divided itself. Those to the right rush down a hill towards a brook with a ford. One or two—men whom he hates with an intensity of envy—have jumped the brook, and have settled to their work. Twenty or thirty others are hustling themselves through the water. The time for a judicious start on that side is already gone. But others—a crowd of others—are facing the big ploughed field immediately before them. That is the straightest riding, and with them he goes. Why has the scent lain so hot over the upturned heavy ground? Why do they go so fast at this, the very first blush of morning? Fortune is always against him, and the horse is pulling him through the mud as though the brute meant to drag his arm out of the socket. At the first fence, as he is steadying himself, a butcher passes him roughly in the jump and nearly takes away the side of his top boot. He is knocked half out of his saddle, and in that condition scrambles through. When he has regained his equilibrium he sees the happy butcher going into the field beyond. He means to curse the butcher when he catches him, but the butcher is safe. A field and a half before him he sees the tail hounds, and renews his effort. He has meant to like it today, and he will. So he rides at the next fence boldly, where the butcher has left his mark, and does it pretty well—with a slight struggle. Why is it that he can never get over a ditch without some struggle in his saddle, some scramble with his horse? Why does he curse the poor animal so constantly—unless it be that he cannot catch the butcher? Now he rushes at a gate which others have opened for him, but he rushes too late and catches his leg. Mad with pain, he nearly gives it up, but the spark of pluck is still there, and with throbbing knee he perseveres. How he hates it! It is all detestable now. He cannot hold his horse because of his gloves, and he cannot get them off. The sympathetic beast knows that his master is unhappy, and makes himself unhappy and troublesome in consequence. Our friend is still going, riding wildly, but still keeping a grain of caution for his fences. He has not been down yet, but has barely saved himself more than once. The ploughs are very deep, and his horse, though still boring at him, pants heavily. Oh, that there might come a check, or that the brute of a fox might happily go to ground! But no! The ruck of the hunt is far away from him in front, and the game is running steadily straight for some well known though still distant protection. But the man who doesn't like it still sees a red coat before him, and perseveres in chasing the wearer of it. The solitary red coat becomes distant, and still more distant from him, but he goes on while he can yet keep the line in which the red coat has ridden. He must hurry himself, however, or he will be lost to humanity, and will be alone. He must hurry himself, but his horse now desires to hurry no more. So he puts the spurs to the brute savagely, and then at some little fence, some ignoble ditch, they come down together in the mud, and the question of any further effort is saved for the rider. When he arises the red coat is out of sight, and his own horse is half across the field before him. In such a position, is it possible that a man should like it?

About four o'clock in the afternoon, when the other men are coming in, he turns up at the hunting stables, and nobody asks him any questions. He may have been doing fairly well for what anybody knows, and, as he says nothing of himself, his disgrace is at any rate hidden. Why should he tell that he had been nearly an hour on foot trying to catch his horse, that he had sat himself down on a bank and almost cried, and that he had drained his flask to the last drop before one o'clock? No one need know the extent of his miseries. And no one does know how great is the misery endured by those who hunt regularly, and who do not like it.

"The Grand National" from National Velvet

[ENID BAGNOLD]

Well, first here's a map of the Course. I got it from a chap. You oughta walked round with me this morning but it's so wet an' if I get you tired you'll be no use. Besides, it's best you do without seeing what the other side o' Becher's is like."

"When did you see it?"

"When did I see it? Didn't I tell you I know it all up here like my thumb? One time I used to shift coal on trucks on the line alongside Becher's. You can't see much on the National, there's such a crowd, but the Liverpool Autumn Meeting in November you got all to yourself. You can stand up there an' see the ambulance come an' see the men standing there with ropes ready an' all."

"Ooh, Mi, ready for what?"

"Ready to lug the horses out of the drop."

"Ooh—Mi."

"Huh! It's not going to happen to you! You got The Piebald jumping under you. Don't you forget that. All I mean is don't be surprised when you ride at Becher's, an' don't think you've jumped over the lip of a quarry, 'cos it isn't a quarry and you'll stop dropping in the end an' if you're not surprised the horse won't be."

"Yes, Mi."

"Now. We'll take the jumps all round. Same as if you were walking round, which you should be."

Mi pulled his chair up to Velvet's bed and flattened the thin paper map on her sheet.

"Plan of the Liverpool Racecourse," it said. "Distance of Grand National Course about four miles 856 yards."

"Now then," said Mi. "Just listen. You start. . . . *here* at the corner. It says 'Paddock' just behind."

"Yes, Mi."

"(An don' keep saying, 'Yes, Mi.' Don't fuss too much about your start. It's no odds getting off in a tear-away. What you got to do is to jump round and jump clean and go as fas as you can when you know what you're doing. But wait till you know what you're doing before you hurry. Mind you, he doesn't know nothing about racing. He won't be hard to hold. I know you got him under your thumb. Now. . . . First you cross a road. On tan. The tan'll fly up in your eye. Keep 'em shut across the road. Then the first fence. Plain fence. Then the next. Plain fence. You done just as big in the mushroom valley. There's nothing in them, but don't you despise 'em. Many's come down in the first two. There won't be much tailing there. You'll be all clustered up.

"Then comes a rail, ditch, and fence. I'm not saying it isn't an awful whopper for them as stands at the sides an' looks. It looks awful from the truck-way. But it won't look so bad to you, you won't know it. You'll see a yellow-looking log lying low on the ground and you must take off in time before it. It's on the lip of the ditch. It's not the landing so much there as the take-off.

"Then there's two more thorn fences. Then there's Becher's.

"Now *there's no need to fall at Becher's*. No need at all. I watched it an' I know. If I was sitting below you on the far side I wouldn't want to see the eyes popping out of your head as you came down. Just sit back. If you lie back you'll only be upright to the ground. Don't jerk his head whatever you do. It's a long way down but he'll land steady. Just keep as still as if you were a dummy, and put confidence into him."

"What's the drop, Mi?"

"I don' know but it looks twenty. On account of the ditch at the bottom. But you clear the ditch.

That's nothing to do with you. You land on uphill grass an' gallop on. Then there's a . . . (I can't read that one! It's printed on the black. It's a plain jump anyway.). Then there's the Canal Turn. . . . "

"Mi, I can't remember it all!"

"Put yer mind to it. The Canal Turn's a teaser. You got to put yer mind to it. There's a chance of horses running out there. They got a screen up to stop it but they seem to want to run out to the left. There's the canal shinin' right ahead. Perhaps that's it. They don't want to swim.

"You want to make for the middle of the jump at the Canal Turn. Don't you go skidding in to the left and saving ground. If you get on the inside as they turn an' you've just landed, God help you. Even if you can't remember anything else remember to keep to the middle at the Canal Turn. You can't go wrong. There's the canal shinin' just in front of you. A pack of seagull's'll rise most likely as you come up. They always do."

"Mi, I swear I can't remember any more."

"But I gotta tell you about Valentine's. . . . Even if I drop the rest of the jumps I gotta tell you it's twice around the Course."

"Well, go on. But not about the jumps. Yes . . . tell me about the water jump."

"The water jump's pink," said Mi despondently.

"How d'you mean?"

"You got to say to yourself, 'It's pink. I gotta jump all of the pink.'"

"Why's it pink?"

"Everything else is grey," said Mi, dully. "The water's puddled on pink clay. It looks meaty. It's opposite the Grand Stand. The people'll be yelling."

"Go on, Mi! Tell me some more!"

"Look here now, I talked to a lotta chaps. This is how it is. Them jumps in the valley you gather yer horse up, don't you?"

"Yes."

"Well, you can't go on doing that twice roun' the National. Or if you do you gotta do it like silk. 'Cos when a horse gets as done as that he can't stand being gathered up, not like you would at the beginning. You gotta haul him in. You remember that! You gotta haul him in 's though he . . . .'s though he was a big fish that was on'y half hooked. When he gets on to the Racecourse. . . ."

"At the beginning?"

"No . . . that's what they call the end. The Racecourse. It means getting on to the straight after the jumps. It's when you get off the National Course an' come galloping up on the Gold Cup Course just before the Grand Stand. They call it 'coming on to the Racecourse.'"

"Yes, Mi. Yes . . . well, I mean?"

"What was I saying? Oh, yes. When the horses get on to the second round, or a bit after (some don't do it till the second time Becher's), they begin to get their necks stickin' out so far you wouldn't know 'em. They can't jump like that. On the other hand if you pull 'em in with a jerk you throw 'em down. You want to haul. You want to take a pull an' a pull, 's gentle 's through you got 'em on a piece of silk an' it'll break. You gotta judge yourself how much you'll hustle after you've landed an' how soon before the next you'll take a little swig at the hauling."

Blue Murder

[WILBUR DANIEL STEELE]

At Mill Crossing it was already past sunset. The rays, redder for what autumn leaves were left, still laid fire along the woods crowning the stony slopes of Jim Bluedge's pastures; but then the line of the dusk began and from that level it filled the valley, washing with transparent blue the buildings scattered about the bridge, Jim's house and horse sheds and hay barns, Frank's store, and Camden's blacksmith shop.

The mill had been gone fifty years, but the falls which had turned its wheel still poured in the bottom of the valley, and when the wind came from the Footstool way their mist wet the smithy, built of the old stone on the old foundations, and their pouring drowned the clink of Camden's hammer.

Just now they couldn't drown Camden's hammer, for he wasn't in the smithy; he was at his brother's farm. Standing inside the smaller of the horse paddocks behind the sheds, he drove in stakes, one after another, cut green from saplings, and so disposed as to cover the more glaring of the weaknesses in the five foot fence. From time to time, when one was done and another to do, he rested the head of his sledge in the pocket of his leather apron (he was never without it; it was as though it had grown on him, lumpy with odds and ends of his trade—bolts and nails and rusty pliers and old horseshoes) and, standing so, he mopped the sweat from his face and looked up at the mountain.

Of the three brothers he was the dumb one. He seldom had anything to say. It was providential (folks said) that of the three enterprises at the Crossing one was a smithy; for while he was a strong, big, hungry-muscled fellow, he never would have had the shrewdness to run the store or the farm. He was better at pounding—pounding while the fire reddened and the sparks flew, and thinking, and letting other people wonder what he was thinking of.

Blossom Bluedge, his brother's wife, sat perched on the top bar of the paddock gate, holding her skirts around her ankles with a trifle too much care to be quite unconscious, and watched him work. When he looked at the mountain he was looking at the mares, half a mile up the slope, grazing in a line as straight as soldiers, their heads all one way. But Blossom thought it was the receding light he was thinking of, and her own sense of misgiving returned and deepened.

"You'd have thought Jim would be home before this, wouldn't you, Cam?"

Her brother-in-law said nothing.

"Cam, look at me!"

It was nervousness, but it wasn't all nervousness— she was the prettiest girl in the valley; a small part of it was mingled coquetry and pique.

The smith began to drive another stake, swinging the hammer from high overhead, his muscles play-ing in fine big rhythmical convulsions under the skin of his arms and chest, covered with short blond down. Studying him cornerwise, Blossom muttered, "Well, *don't* look at me, then!"

He was too dumb for any use. He was as dumb as this: When all three of the Bluedge boys were after her a year ago, Frank, the storekeeper, had brought her candy; chocolates wrapped in silver foil in a two-pound Boston box. Jim had laid before her the Bluedge farm and with it the dominance of the val-ley. And Camden! To the daughter of Ed Beck, the apple grower, Camden brought a *box of apples*!—and been bewildered too, when, for all she could help it, she had had to clap a hand over her mouth and run into the house to have her giggle.

A little more than just bewildered, perhaps. Had she, or any of them, ever speculated about that? He had been dumb enough before; but that was when he started being as dumb as he was now.

Well, if he wanted to be dumb 'let him be dumb. Pouting her pretty lips and arching her fine brows, she forgot the unimaginative fellow and turned to the ridge again. And now, seeing the sun was quite gone, all the day's vague worries and dreads—held off by this and that—could not be held off much longer. For weeks there had been so much talk, so much gossip and speculation and doubt.

"Camden," she reverted suddenly. "Tell me one thing. Did you hear—"

She stopped there. Some people were coming into the kitchen yard, dark forms in the growing darkness. Most of them lingered at the porch, sitting on the steps and lighting their pipes. The one that came out was Frank, the second of her brothers-in-law. She was glad. Frank wasn't like Camden; he would talk. Turning and taking care of her skirts, she gave him a bright and sisterly smile.

"Well, Frankie, what's the crowd?"

Far from avoiding the smile, as Camden's habit was, the storekeeper returned it with a brotherly wink for good measure. "Oh, they're tired of waiting down the road, so they come up here to see the grand arrival." He was something of a man of the world; in his calling he acquired a fine turn for skepticism. "Don't want to miss being on hand to see what flaws they can pick in 'Jim's five hundred dollars' worth of experiment.'"

"Frank, ain't you the least bit worried over Jim? So late?"

"Don't see why."

"All the same, I wish either you or Cam could've gone with him."

"Don't see why. Had all the men from Perry's stable there in Twinshead to help him get the animal off the freight, and he took an extra rope and the log-chain and the heavy wagon, so I guess no matter how wild and woolly the devil is he'll scarcely be climbing over the tailboard. Besides, them Western horses ain't such a big breed; even a stallion."

"All the same—(look the other way, Frankie)." Flipping her ankles over the rail, Blossom jumped down beside him.

"Listen, Frank, tell me something. Did you hear— did you hear the reason Jim's getting him cheap was because he killed a man out West there, what's-its-name, Wyoming?"

Frank was taking off his sleeve protectors, the pins in his mouth. It was Camden, at the bars, speaking in his sudden deep rough way: "Who the hell told you that?"

Frank got the pins out of his mouth. "I guess what it is, Blossie, what's mixed you up is his having that name 'Blue Murder.' "

"No sir! I got some sense and some ears. You don't go fooling me."

Frank laughed indulgently and struck her shoulder with a light hand.

"Don't worry. Between two horsemen like Jim and Cam—"

"Don't *Cam* me! He's none of *my* horse. I told Jim once—" Breaking off, Camden hoisted his weight over the fence and stood outside, his feet spread and his hammer in both hands, an attitude that would have looked a little ludicrous had anyone been watching him.

Jim had arrived. With a clatter of hoofs and a rattle of wheels he was in the yard and come to a standstill, calling aloud as he threw the lines over the team, "Well, friends, here we are."

The curious began to edge around, closing a cautious circle. The dusk had deepened so that it was hard to make anything at any distance of Jim's "experiment" but a blurry silhouette anchored at the wagon's tail. The farmer put an end to it, crying from his eminence, "Now, now, clear out and don't worry him; give him some peace tonight, for Lord's sake! Git!" He jumped to the ground and began to whack his arms, chilled with driving, only to have them pinioned by Blossom's without warning.

"Oh, Jim, I'm so glad you come. I been so worried; gi' me a kiss!"

The farmer reddened, eyeing the cloud of witnesses. He felt awkward and wished she could have waited. "Get along, didn't I tell you fellows?" he cried with a trace of the Bluedge temper. "Go and wait in the kitchen then; I'll tell you all about everything soon's I come in. . . . Well now—wife—"

"What's the matter?" she laughed, an eye over her shoulder. "Nobody's looking that matters. I'm sure Frank don't mind. And as for Camden—"

Camden wasn't looking at them. Still standing with his hammer two-fisted and his legs spread, his chin down and his thoughts to himself (the dumb head) he was looking at Blue Murder, staring at that other dumb head, which, raised high on the motionless column of the stallion's neck, seemed hearkening with an exile's doubt to the new sounds of this new universe, testing with wide nostrils the taint in the wind of equine strangers, and studying with eyes accustomed to far horizons these dark pastures that went up in the air.

Whatever the smith's cogitations, presently he let the hammer down and said aloud, "So you're him, eh?"

Jim put Blossom aside, saying "Got supper ready? I'm hungry!" Excited by the act of kissing and the sense of witnesses to it, she fussed with her hair and started kitchenwards as he turned to his brothers.

"Well, what do you make of him?"

"Five hundred dollars," said Frank. "However, it's your money."

Camden was shorter. "Better put him in."

"All right; let them bars down while I and Frank lead him around."

"No thanks!" The storekeeper kept his hands in his pockets. "I just cleaned up, thanks. Cam's the boy for horses."

"He's none o' my horse!" Camden wet his lips, shook his shoulders, and scowled. "Be damned, no!" He never had the right words, and it made him mad. Hadn't he told Jim from the beginning that he washed his hands of this fool Agricultural College squandering, "and a man-killer to the bargain?"

"Unless," Frank put in slyly, "unless Cam's scared."

"Oh, is Cam scared?"

"Scared?" And still to the brothers' enduring wonder, the big dense fellow would rise to that boyhood bait. "Scared? The hell I'm scared of any horse ever wore a shoe! Come on, I'll show you! I'll show you!"

"Well, be gentle with him, boys, he may be brittle." As Frank sauntered off around the shed he whistled the latest tune.

In the warmth and light of the kitchen he began to fool with his pretty sister-in-law, feigning princely impatience and growling with a wink at the assembled neighbors, "When do we eat?"

But she protested, "Land, I had everything ready since five, ain't I? And now if it ain't you it's them to wait for. I declare for men!"

At last one of the gossips got in a word.

"What you make of Jim's purchase, Frank?"

"Well, it's Jim's money, Darred. If *I* had the running of this farm——" Frank began drawing up chairs noisily, leaving it at that.

Darred persisted. "Don't look to me much like an animal for women and children to handle, not yet awhile."

"Cowboys han'les 'em, pa." That was Darred's ten-year-old, big-eyed.

Blossom put the kettle back, protesting, "Leave off, or you'll get me worried to death; all your talk. . . . I declare, where *are* those bad boys?" Opening the door, she called into the dark, "Jim! Cam! Land's sake!"

Subdued by distance and the intervening sheds, she could hear them at their business—sounds, muffled and fragmentary, soft thunder of hoofs, snorts, puffings, and the short words of men in action: "Aw, leave him be in the paddock tonight.". . . "With them mares there, you damn fool?". . . .

"Damn fool, eh? Try getting him in at that door and see who's the damn fool!".... "Come on, don't be so scared".... "Scared, eh? Scared?"

Why was it she always felt that curious tightening of all her powers of attention when Camden Bluedge spoke? Probably because he spoke so rarely, and then so roughly, as if his own thickness made him mad. Never mind.

"Last call for supper in the dining car, boys!" she called and closed the door. Turning back to the stove, she was about to replace the tea water for the third time when, straightening up, she said, "What's that?"

No one else had heard anything. They looked at one another.

"Frank, go—go see what—go tell the boys to come in."

Frank hesitated, feeling foolish, then went to the door.

Then everyone in the room was out of his chair.

There were three sounds. The first was human and incoherent. The second was incoherent, too, but it wasn't human. The third was a crash, a ripping and splintering of wood.

When they got to the paddock they found Camden crawling from beneath the wreckage of the fence where a gap was opened on the pasture side. He must have received a blow on the head, for he seemed dazed. He didn't seem to know they were there. At a precarious balance—one hand at the back of his neck—he stood facing up the hill, gaping after the diminuendo of floundering hoofs, invisible above.

So seconds passed. Again the beast gave tongue, a high wild horning note, and on the black of the stony hill to the right of it a faint shower of sparks blew like fireflies where the herding mares wheeled. It seemed to awaken the dazed smith. He opened his mouth. "*Almighty God!*" Swinging, he flung his arms towards the shed. *"There! There!"*

At least someone brought a lantern. They found Jim Bluedge lying on his back in the corner of the paddock near the door to the shed. In the lantern light, and still better in the kitchen when they had carried him in, they read the record of the thing which Camden, dumb in good earnest now, seemed unable to tell them with anything but his strange unfocused stare.

The bloody offense to the skull would have been enough to kill the man, but it was the second, full on the chest above the heart, that told the tale. On the caved grating of the ribs, already turning blue under the yellowish down, the iron shoe had left its mark; and when, laying back the rag of shirt, they saw that the toe of the shoe was upward and the cutting calkends down, they knew all they wanted to know of that swift, black, crushing episode.

No outlash of heels in fright. Here was a forefoot. An attack aimed and frontal; an onslaught reared, erect; beast turned biped; red eyes mad to white eyes aghast. . . . And only afterward, when it was done, the blood-fright that serves the horse for conscience; the blind rush down the enclosure; the fence gone down. . . .

No one had much to say. No one seemed to know what to do.

As for Camden, he was no help. He simply stood propped on top of his logs of legs where someone had left him. From the instant when with his *"Almighty God!"* he had been brought back to memory, instead of easing its hold as the minutes passed, the event to which he remained the only living human witness seemed minute by minute to tighten its grip. It set its sweat-beaded stamp on his face, distorted his eyes, and tied his tongue. He was no good to anyone.

As for Blossom, even now—perhaps more than ever now—her dependence on physical touch was the thing that ruled her. Down on her knees beside the lamp they had set on the floor, she plucked at one of the dead man's shoes monotonously, and as it were, idly, swaying the toe like an inverted pendulum from side to side. That was all. Not a word. And when Frank, the only one of the three with any sense, got her up finally and led her away to her room, she clung to *him*.

It was lucky that Frank was a man of affairs. His brother was dead, and frightfully dead, but there was tomorrow for grief. Just now there were many things to do. There were people to be gotten rid of. With short words and angry gestures he cleared them out, all but Darred and a man named White, and to these he said, "Now first thing, Jim can't stay here." He ran and got a blanket from a closet. "Give me a hand and we'll lay him in the ice house overnight. Don't sound so good, but it's best, poor fellow. Cam, come along!"

He waited a moment, and as he studied the wooden fool the blood poured back into his face. "Wake up, Cam! You great big scared stiff, you!"

Camden brought his eyes out of nothingness and looked at his brother. A twinge passed over his face, convulsing the mouth muscles. "Scared?"

"Yes, you're scared!" Frank's lip lifted, showing the tips of his teeth. "And I'll warrant you something; if you wasn't the scared stiff you was, this hellish damn thing wouldn't have happened, maybe. Scared! You a blacksmith! Scared of a horse!"

"*Horse!*" Again that convulsion of the mouth muscles, something between irony and an idiot craft. "Why don't you go catch 'im?"

"Hush it! Don't waste time by going loony now, for God's sake. Come!"

"My advice to anybody—" Camden looked crazier than ever, knotting his brows—"my advice to anybody is to let somebody else go catch that—that—" Opening the door, he faced out into the night, his head sunk between his shoulders and the fingers working at the ends of his hanging arms; and before they knew it he began to swear. They could hardly hear because his teeth were locked and his breath soft. There were all the vile words he had ever heard in his life, curses and threats and abominations, vindictive, violent, obscene. He stopped only when at a sharp word from Frank he was made aware that Blossom had come back into the room. Even then he didn't seem to comprehend her return but stood blinking at her, and at the rifle she carried, with his distraught bloodshot eyes.

Frank comprehended. Hysteria had followed the girl's blankness. Stepping between her and the body on the floor, he spoke in a persuasive, unhurried way. "What are you doing with that gun, Blossie? Now, now, you don't want that gun, you know you don't."

It worked. Her rigidity lessened appreciably. Confusion gained.

"Well, but—oh, Frank—well but, when we going to shoot him?"

"Yes, yes, Blossie—now, yes—only you best give me that gun, that's the girlie."

When he had got the weapon he put an arm around her shoulders. "Yes, yes 'course we're going to shoot him; what you think? Don't want an animal like that running round. Now first thing in the morning—"

Hysteria returned. With its strength she resisted his leading.

"No, now! *Now!*

"He's gone and killed Jim! Killed my husband! I won't have him left alive another minute! I won't! *Now!* No sir, I'm going myself, I am! Frank, I am! *Cam!*"

At his name, appealed to in that queer screeching way, the man in the doorway shivered all over, wet his lips, and walked out into the dark.

"There, you see?" Frank was quick to capitalize on anything. "Cam's gone to do it. Cam's gone, Blossie! . . . Here, one of you—Darred, take this gun and run, give it to Camden, that's the boy."

"You sure he'll kill him, Frank? You *sure?*"

"Sure as daylight. Now you come along back to your room like a good girl and get some rest. Come, I'll go with you."

When Frank returned to the kitchen ten minutes later, Darred was back.

"Well, now, let's get at it and carry out poor Jim; he can't lay here. . . . Where's Cam gone *now,* damn him!"

"Cam? Why, he's gone and went."

"Went where?"

"Up the pasture, like you said."

"Like I—" Frank went an odd color. He walked to the door. Between the light on the sill and the beginnings of the stars where the woods crowned the mountain was all one blackness. One stillness too. He turned on Darred. "But look, you never gave him that gun, even."

"He didn't want it."

"Lord's sake. What did he say?"

"Said nothing. He'd got the log-chain out of the wagon and when I caught him he was up hunting his hammer in under that wreck at the fence. Once he found it he started off up. 'Cam,' says I, 'here's a gun, want it?' He seem not to. Just when on walking up."

"How'd he look?"

"Look same's you seen him looking. Sick."

"The damned fool!". . .

Poor dead Jim! Poor fool Camden! As the store-keeper went about his business, and afterwards when, the ice-house door closed on its tragic tenant and White and Darred gone off home, he roamed the yard, driven here and there, soft-footed, waiting, hearkening—his mind was for a time not on his own property but the plaything of thoughts diverse and wayward. Jim. His brother, so suddenly and so violently gone. The stallion. That beast that had kicked him to death. With anger and hate and pitiless impatience of time he thought of the morrow, when they would catch him and take their revenge with guns and clubs. Behind these speculations, covering the background of his consciousness and stringing his nerves to endless vigil, spread the wall of the mountain; silent from instant to instant but devising under its black silence (who could know what instant to come) a neigh, a yell, a spark-line of iron hoofs on rolling flints, a groan. And still behind that and deeper into the borders of the unconscious, the storekeeper thought of the farm that had lost its master, the rich bottoms, the broad, well-stocked pastures, the fat barns, and the comfortable house whose chimneys and gable ends fell into changing shapes of perspective against the stars as he wandered here and there. . . .

Jim gone . . . and Camden, at any moment. . . .

His face grew hot. An impulse carried him a dozen steps. "I ought to go up. Ought to take the gun and go up." But there shrewd sanity put on the brakes. "Where's the use? Couldn't find him in the dark. Besides I oughtn't to leave Blossom here alone."

With that he went around towards the kitchen, thinking to go in. But the sight of the lantern, left burning out near the sheds, sent his ideas off on another course. At any rate it would give his muscles and nerves something to work on. Taking the lantern and entering the paddock, he fell to patching the gap into the pasture, using broken boards from the wreck. As he worked his eyes chanced to fall on footprints in the dung-mixed earth—Camden's footprints, leading away beyond the little ring of light. And beside them, taking off from the landing place of that prodigious leap, he discerned the trail of the stallion. After a moment he got down on his knees where the earth was softest, holding the lantern so that its light fell full.

He gave over his fence building. Returning to the house his gait was no longer that of the roamer; his face, caught by the periodic flare of the swinging lantern, was the face of another man. In its expression there was a kind of fright and a kind of calculating eagerness. He looked at the clock on the kitchen shelf, shook it, and read it again. He went to the telephone and fumbled at the receiver. He waited till his hand quit shaking, then removed it from the hook.

"Listen, Darred," he said when he had got the farmer at last, "get White and whatever others you can and come over first thing it's light. Come a-riding and bring your guns. No, Cam ain't back."

He heard Blossom calling. Outside her door he passed one hand down over his face, as he might have passed a wash rag to wipe off what was there. Then he went in.

"What's the matter, Blossie? Can't sleep?"

"No, I can't sleep. Can't think. Can't sleep. Oh, Frankie!"

He sat down beside the bed.

"Oh, Frankie, Frankie, *hold my hand*!"

She looked almost homely, her face bleached out and her hair a mess on the pillow. But she would get over that. And the short sleeve of the nightgown on the arm he held was edged with pretty lace.

"Got your watch here?" he asked. She gave it to him from under the pillow. This too he shook as if he couldn't believe it was going.

Pretty Blossom Beck. Here for a wonder he sat in her bedroom and held her hand. One brother was dead and the other was on the mountain.

But little by little, as he sat and dreamed so, nightmare crept over his brain. He had to arouse and shake himself. He had to set his thoughts res-olutely in other roads. . . . Perhaps there would be even the smithy. The smithy, the store, the farm. Complete. The farm, the farmhouse, the room in the farmhouse, the bed in the room, the wife in the bed. Complete beyond belief. If. . . . Worth dodging horror for. If. . . .

"Frank, has Cam come back?"

"Cam? Don't worry about Cam. Where's that watch again?"

Far from rounding up their quarry in the early hours after dawn, it took the riders, five of them, till almost noon simply to make certain that he wasn't to be found—not in any of the pastures. Then when they discovered the hole in the fence far up in the woods beyond the crest where Blue Murder had led the mares in a break for the open country of hills and ravines to the south, they were only beginning.

The farmers had left their work undone at home and, as the afternoon lengthened and with it the shadows in the hollow places, they began to eye one another behind their leader's back. Yet they couldn't say it; there was something in the storekeeper's air today, something zealous and pitiless and fanatical, that shut them up and pulled them plodding on.

Frank did the trailing. Hopeless of getting anywhere before sundown in that unkempt wilderness of a hundred square miles of scrub, his companions slouched in their saddles and rode more and more mechanically, knee to knee, and it was he who made the casts to recover the lost trail and, dismounting to read the dust, cried back, "He's still with 'em," and with gestures of imperious excitement beckoned them on.

"Which you mean?" Darred asked him once. "Cam or the horse?"

Frank wheeled his beast and spurred back at the speaker. It was extraordinary. "You don't know what you're talking about!" he cried, with a causelessness and a disordered vehemence that set them first staring, then speculating. "Come on, you dumb heads; don't talk—*ride*!"

By the following day, when it was being told in all the farmhouses, the story might vary in details and more and more as the tellings multiplied, but in its fundamentals it remained the same. In one thing they certainly all agreed: they used the same expression— "It was like Frank was drove. Drove in a race against something, and not sparing the whip."

They were a good six miles to the south of the fence. Already the road back home would have to be followed three parts in the dark.

Darred was the spokesman. "Frank, I'm going to call it a day."

The others reined up with him but the man ahead rode on. He didn't seem to hear. Darred lifted his voice. "Come on, call it a day, Frank. Tomorrow, maybe. But you see we've run it out and they're not here."

"Wait," said Frank over his shoulder, still riding on into the pocket.

White's mount, a mare, laid back her ears, shied, and stood trembling. After a moment she whinnied.

It was as if she had whinnied for a dozen. A crashing in the woods above them to the left and the avalanche came—down streaming, erupting, wheeling, wheeling away with volleying snorts, a dark rout.

Darred, reining his horse, began to shout, "Here they go this way, Frank!" But Frank was yelling, "Up here, boys! This way, quick!"

It was the same note, excited, feverish, disordered, breaking like a child's. When they neared him they saw he was off his horse, rifle in hand, and down on his knees to study the ground where the woods began. By the time they reached his animal the impetuous fellow had started up into the cover, his voice trailing, "Come on, spread out and come on!"

One of the farmers got down. When he saw the other three keeping their saddles he swung up again.

White spoke this time. "Be darned if I do!" He lifted a protesting hail. "Come back here Frank! You're crazy! It's getting dark!"

It was Frank's own fault. They told him plainly to come back and he wouldn't listen.

For a while they could hear his crackle in the mounting underbrush. Then that stopped, whether he had gone too far for their ears or whether he had come to a halt to give his own ears a chance. . . .

Once, off to the right, a little higher up under the low ceiling of the trees that darkened moment by moment with the rush of night, they heard another movement, another restlessness of leaves and stones. Then that was still, and everything was still.

Darred ran a sleeve over his face and swung down. "God alive, boys!"

It was the silence. All agreed there—the silence and the deepening dusk.

The first they heard was the shot. No voice. Just the one report. Then after five breaths of another silence a crashing of growth, a charge in the darkness under the withered scrub, continuous and diminishing.

They shouted "Frank!" No answer. They called, *"Frank Bluedge!"*

Now, since they had to, they did. Keeping contact by word, and guided partly by directional memory (and mostly in the end by luck), after a time they found the storekeeper in a brake of ferns, lying across his gun.

They got him down to the open, watching behind them all the while. Only then, by the flares of successive matches, under the noses of the snorting horses, did they look for the damage done.

They remembered the stillness and the gloom; it must have been quite black in there. The attack had come from behind—equine and pantherine at once, and planned and cunning. A deliberate lunge with a forefoot again; the shoe which had crushed the backbone between the shoulder blades was a fore shoe; that much they saw by the match flares in the red wreck.

They took no longer getting home than they had to, but it was longer than they wished. With Frank across his own saddle, walking their horses and with one or another ahead to pick the road (it was going to rain, and even the stars were lost), they made no more than a creeping speed.

None of them had much to say on the journey. Finding the break in the boundary fence and feeling through the last of the woods, the lights of their farms began to show in the pool of blackness below, and Darred uttered a part of what had lain in their minds during the return.

"Well, that leaves Cam."

None followed it up. None cared to go any closer than he was to the real question. Something new, alien, menacing and pitiless had come into the valley of their lives with that beast they had never really seen; they felt its oppression, every one, and kept the real question back in their minds: "*Does* it leave Cam?"

It answered itself. Camden was at home when they got there.

He had some in a little before them, empty-handed. Empty-headed, too. When Blossom, who had waited all day, part of the time with neighbor women who had come in and part of the time alone to the point of going mad—when she saw him coming down the pasture, his feet stumbling and his shoulders dejected, her first feeling was relief. Her first words, however, were "Did you get him, Cam?" And all he would answer was, "Gi' me something to eat, can't you? Gi' me a few hours' sleep, can't you? Then wait!"

He looked as if he would need more than a few hours' sleep. Propped on his elbows over his plate, it seemed as though his eyes would close before his mouth would open.

His skin was scored by thorns and his shirt was in ribbons under the straps of his iron-sagged apron; but it was not by these marks that his twenty-odd hours showed; it was by his face. While yet his eyes were open and his wits still half awake, his face surrendered. The flesh relaxed into lines of stupor, a putty-formed, putty-colored mask of sleep.

Once he let himself be aroused. This was when, to an abstracted query as to Frank's whereabouts, Blossom told him Frank had been out with four others since dawn. He heaved clear of the table and opened his eyes at her, showing the red around the rims.

He spoke with the thick tongue of the drunkard. "If anybody but me lays hand on that stallion, I'll kill him. I'll wring his neck."

Then he relapsed into his stupidity, and not even the arrival of the party bringing his brother's body home seemed able to shake him so far clear of it again.

At first, when they had laid Frank on the floor where on the night before they had laid Jim, he seemed hardly to comprehend.

"What's wrong with Frank?"

"Some more of Jim's 'experiment.'"

"Frank see him? He's scared, Frank is. Look at his face there."

"He's dead, Cam."

"Dead, you say? Frank dead? Dead of fright; is that it?"

Even when, rolling the body over they showed him what was what, he appeared incapable of comprehension, of amazement, of passion, or of any added grief. He looked at them all with a kind of befuddled protest. Returning to his chair and his plate, he grumbled, "Le' me eat first, can't you? Can't you gi' me a little time to sleep?"

"Well, you wouldn't do much tonight anyway, I guess."

At White's words Blossom opened her mouth for the first time.

"No, nothing tonight, Cam. Cam! *Camden!* Say! Promise!"

"And then tomorrow, Cam, what we'll do is get every last man in the valley, and we'll go at this right. We'll lay hand on that devil—"

Camden swallowed his mouthful of cold steak with difficulty. His obsession touched, he showed them the rims of his eyes again.

"You do and I'll wring your necks. The man that touches that animal before I do gets his neck wrang. That's all you need to remember."

"Yes, yes—no—that is—" Poor Blossom. "Yes, Mr. White, thanks; no, Cam's not going out tonight. . . . No, Cam, nobody's going to interfere—nor nothing. Don't you worry there. . . . "

Again poor Blossom! Disaster piled too swiftly on disaster; no discipline but instinct left. Caught in fire and flood and earthquake and not knowing what to come, and no creed but "save him who can!"—by hook or crook of wile or smile. With the valley of her life emptied out, and its emptiness repeopled monstrously and pressing down black on the roof under which (now that Frank was gone to the ice house too and the farmers back home) one brother was left of three—she would tread softly, she would talk or she would be dumb, as her sidelong glimpses of the awake-asleep man's face above the table told her was the instant's need; or if he would eat, she would magic out of nothing something, anything;

or if he would sleep, he could sleep, so long as he slept in that house where she could know he was sleeping.

Only one thing. If she could touch him. If she could touch and cling.

Lightning filled the windows. After a moment the thunder came avalanching down the pasture and brought up against the clapboards of the house. At this she was behind his chair. She put out a hand. She touched his shoulder. The shoulder was bare, the shirt ripped away; it was caked with sweat and with the blackening smears of scratches, but for all its exhaustion it was flesh alive—a living man to touch.

Camden blundered up. "What the hell!" He started off two steps and wheeled on her. "Why don't you get off to bed for Goll sake!"

"Yes, Cam, yes—right off, yes."

"Well, *I'm* going, I can tell you. For Goll sake, I need some sleep!"

"Yes, that's right, yes, Cam, good night, Cam— only—only you promise—promise you won't go out—nowheres."

"Go *out*? Not likely I won't! Not *likely*! Get along."

It took her no time to get going then—quick and quiet as a mouse.

Camden lingered to stand at one of the windows where the lightning came again, throwing the black barns and paddocks at him from the white sweep of the pastures crowned by woods.

As it had taken her no time to go, it took Blossom no time to undress and get in bed. When Camden was on his way to his room he heard her calling, "Cam! Just a second, Cam!"

In the dark outside her door he drew one hand down over his face, wiping off whatever might be there. Then he entered.

"Yes? What?"

"Cam, set by me a minute, won't you? And Cam, oh Cam, hold my hand."

As he slouched down, his fist enclosing her fingers, thoughts awakened and ran and fastened on things. They fastened, tentatively at first, upon the farm. Jim gone. Frank gone. The smithy, the store, and the farm. The whole of Mill Crossing. The trinity. The three in one. . . .

"Tight, Cam, for pity's sake! Hold it tight!"

His eyes, falling to his fist, strayed up along the arm it held. The sleeve, rumpled near the shoulder, was trimmed with pretty lace. . . .

"Tighter, Cam!"

A box of apples. That memory hidden away in the cellar of his mind. Hidden away, clamped down in the dark, till the noxious vapors, the murderous vapors of its rotting had filled the shut-up house he was. . . . A box of red apples for the apple grower's girl. . . . the girl who sniggered and ran away from him to laugh at him. . . .

And here, by the unfolding of a devious destiny, he sat in that girl's bedroom, holding that girl's hand. Jim who had got her, Frank who had wanted her, lay side by side out there in the ice house under the lightning. While he, the "dumb one"—the last to be thought of with anything but amusement and the last to be feared—his big hot fist enclosing her imprecating hand now, and his eyes on the pretty lace at her shoulder—He jumped up with a gulp and a clatter of iron.

"What the—" He flung her hand away. "What the—hell!" He swallowed. "Damn you, Blossie Beck!" He stared at her with repugnance and mortal fright. "Why, you—you-you—"

He moderated his voice with an effort, wiping his brow. "Good night. You must excuse me, Blossie. I wasn't meaning—I mean—I hope you sleep good. *I* shall. Good night!"

In his own brain was the one word "Hurry!"

She lay and listened to his boots going along the hall and heard the closing of his door. She ought to have put out the lamp. But even with the shades drawn, the lightning around the edges of the window unnerved her; in the dark alone it would have been more than she could bear.

She lay so still she felt herself nearing exhaustion from the sustained rigidity of her limbs. Rain came and with the rain, wind. Around the eaves it neighed like wild stallions; down the chimneys it moaned like men.

Slipping out of bed and pulling on a bathrobe she ran from her room, barefooted, and along the hall to Camden's door.

"Cam!" she called. "Oh, Cam!" she begged. "Please, please!"

And now he wouldn't answer her.

New lightning, diffused through all the sky by the blown rain, ran at her along the corridor. She pushed the door open. The lamp was burning on the bureau but the room was empty and the bed untouched.

Taking the lamp she skittered down to the kitchen. No one was there. . . .

"Hurry!"

Camden had reached the woods when the rain came. Lighting the lantern he had brought, he made his way on to the boundary fence. There, about a mile to the east of the path the others had taken that day, he pulled the rails down and tumbled the stones together in a pile. Then he proceeded another hundred yards, holding the lantern high and peering through the streaming crystals of the rain.

Blue Murder was there. Neither the chain nor the sapling had given way. The lantern and, better than the lantern, a globe of lightning, showed the tethered stallion glistening and quivering, his eyes all whites at the man's approach.

"Gentle, boy; steady, boy!" Talking all the while in the way he had with horses, Camden put a hand on the taut chain and bore with a gradually progressive weight, bringing the dark head nearer. "Steady, boy; gentle there, damn you; gentle!"

Was he afraid of horses? Who said he was afraid of horses?

The beast's head was against the man's chest, held there by an arm thrown over the bowed neck. As he smoothed the forehead and fingered the nose with false caresses, Camden's "horse talk" ran on—the cadence one thing, the words another.

"Steady, Goll damn you; you're going to get yours. Cheer up, cheer up, the worst is yet to come. Come now! Come easy! Come along!"

When he had unloosed the chain, he felt for and found with his free hand his hammer hidden behind the tree. Throwing the lantern into the brush where it flared for an instant before dying, he led the stallion back as far as the break he had made in the fence. Taking a turn with the chain around the animal's nose, like an improvised hackamore, he swung from the stone pile to the slippery back. A moment's shying, a sliding caracole of amazement and distrust, a crushing of knees, a lash of the chain end, and that was all there was to that. Blue Murder had been ridden before. . . .

In the smithy, chambered in the roaring of the falls and the swish and shock of the storm, Camden sang as he pumped his bellows, filling the cave beneath the rafters with red. The air was nothing, the words were mumbo-jumbo, but they swelled his chest. His eyes, cast from time to time at his wheeling prisoner had lost their look of helplessness and surly distraction.

Scared? He? No, no, no! Now that he wasn't any longer afraid of time, he wasn't afraid of anything on earth.

"Shy, you devil!" He wagged his exalted head. "Whicker, you hellion! Whicker all you want to, stud horse! Tomorrow they're going to get you, the numb fools! Tomorrow they can have you. *I* got you *tonight!*"

He was more than other men; he was enormous. Fishing an iron shoe from that inseparable apron pocket of his, he thrust it into the coals and blew and blew. He tried it and it was burning red. He tried it again and it was searing white. Taking it out on the anvil he began to beat it, swinging his hammer one-handed, gigantic. So in the crimson light, irradiating iron sparks, he was at his greatest. Pounding, pounding. A man in the dark of night with a hammer about him can do wonders; with a horse-shoe about him he can cover up a sin. And if the dark of night in a paddock won't hold it, then the dark of undergrowth on a mountainside will. . . .

Pounding, pounding; thinking, thinking in a great halo of hot stars. Feeding his hungry, his insatiable muscles.

"Steady, now, you blue bastard! Steady, boy!"

What he did not realize in his feverish exhaustion was that his muscles were not insatiable. In the thirty-odd hours past they had had a feast spread before them and they had had their fill . . . More than their fill.

As with the scorching iron in his tongs he approached the stallion, he had to step over the nail box he had stepped over five thousand times in the routine of every day.

A box of apples, eh? Apples to snigger at, eh? But whose girl are you now? . . . Scared, eh?

His foot was heavier of a sudden than it should have been. This five thousand and first time, by the drag of the tenth of an inch, the heel caught the lip of the nail box.

He tried to save himself from stumbling. At the same time, instinctively, he held the iron flame in his tongs away.

There was a scream out of a horse's throat; a whiff of hair and burnt flesh.

There was a lash of something in the red shadows. There was another sound and another wisp of stench. . . .

When, guided by the stallion's whinnying, they found the smith next day, they saw by the cant of his head that his neck was broken, and they perceived that he too had on him the mark of a shoe. It lay up on one side of his throat and the broad of a cheek. It wasn't blue, this time, however—it was red. It took them some instants in the sunshine pouring through the wide door the comprehend this phenomenon. It wasn't sunk in by a blow this time; it was burned in, a brand.

Darred called them to look at the stallion, chained behind the forge.

"Almighty God!" The words sounded funny in his mouth. They sounded the funnier in that they were the same ones the blundering smithy had uttered when, staring uphill from his clever wreckage of the paddock fence, he had seen the mares striking sparks from the stones where the stallion struck none. And he, of all men, a smith!

"Almighty God!" called Darred. "What do you make of these here feet?"

One fore hoof was freshly pared for shoeing; the other three hoofs were as virgin as any yearling's on the plains. Blue Murder had never yet been shod. . . .

"The Colonel's Cup" from Memoirs of a Fox-Hunting Man

[SIEGFRIED SASSOON]

The sun was still shining when I got to the course; but it was now less easy to believe that I had engaged myself to contribute to the entertainment which was attracting such a crowd of cheerful country folk. I felt extraneous and forlorn. Everyone else seemed intent on having as good a time as possible on such a lovely afternoon. I had come briskly out from Downfield on a two-horse *char-à-banc* which was waiting outside the station. The journey cost half a crown. Several of my fellow passengers were "bookies" and their clerks, with their name boards and giant umbrellas; their jocosities accentuated the crudity of the impact on my mind made by the realistic atmosphere of racing. I did my best to feel as much like a "gentleman rider" as I could, and to forget that I was making my first appearance in a race.

The air smelt of trodden turf as I lugged my bag (loaded with fourteen one-pound lead weights) into the dressing room, which was in a farm building under some elms on the crest of the rising ground which overlooked the sparsely flagged course. After dumping the bag in a corner of the dry-mud floored barn, I went out to look for Cockbird and Dixon. They were nowhere to be seen, so I returned to the dressing room, reminding myself that Dixon had said he wouldn't bring "our horse" out there any earlier than he was obliged to, since it would only excite him; I also realized that I should get "rattled" myself unless I kept quiet and reserved my energies for three o'clock.

The first race was run at two, and mine was the third event on the card, so I bought that absorbing document and perched myself on an old corn bin to peruse it. "*Riders are requested to return their number-cloths to the Clerk of the Scales immediately after each race.*" I had forgotten that number-cloths existed, so that was news to me. "*These Steeplechases are held subject to National Hunt Rules as to corrupt and fraudulent practices.*" A moment's reflection convinced me that I need not worry about that admonition; it was sufficiently obvious that I had a clean sheet under National Hunt Rules, though it flattered me to feel that I was at least within their jurisdiction.

After these preliminaries, I looked inside the card at the entries. Good heavens, there were fourteen in my race! Several of the names I didn't know. Captain Silcock's "Crumpet." Mr. F. Duckwith's "Grasshopper." Those must be the soldiers who hunted from Downfield. Mr. G. Bagwell's "Kilgrubbin III." That might be—yes, of course, it was—the fat little man on the weedy chestnut, who was always refusing small timber out hunting. Not much danger from him as long as I kept well out of his way at the first fence, and probably he, and several of the others, wouldn't go to the post after all. My own name looked nice.

A blue-jowled man in a yellow waistcoat hurried in, exclaiming, "Can anybody lend me a weight-cloth?" I glanced at my bag and resolved that nothing would induce me to lend him mine (which had yet to receive its baptismal installment of sweat). Several riders were now preparing for the first race, but no one took any notice of me until ginger-haired Roger Pomfret came in. He had been inspecting the fences, and he wiped his fleshy red face with his sleeve as he sat down and started rummaging in his bag. Tentatively, I asked him what he thought of the course. I was quite glad to see someone I knew, though I'd have preferred to see someone else. He chucked me a surly nod, which he supplemented with—"Course? I don't mind telling you, this something course would break the heart of a blank buffalo. It's nothing but twists and turns, and there isn't a something fence you could go fast at without risking your something neck, and a nice hope I've got on that blank sketchy jumper of Brandwick's!"

Before I could think of an answer his boon companion in blasphemy, Bill Jaggett, came in (embellished with a brown billycock hat and black and white check breeches). Jaggett began chaffing him about the something unhealthy ride he was going to have in the Heavy Weights. "I'll lay you a tenner to a fiver you don't get round without falling," he guffawed. Pomfret took the bet and called him a pimply faced bastard into the bargain.

I thought I might as well get dressed up; when I had pulled my boots on and was very deliberately tucking the straps in with the boot hook, Stephen strolled in; he was already wearing his faded pink cap, and the same elongated and anxious countenance which I had seen a year ago. No doubt my own face matched his. When we'd reassured one another about the superlative fitness of our horses he asked if I'd had any lunch, and as I hadn't he produced a bar of chocolate and an orange, which I was glad to get. Stephen was always thoughtful of other people.

The shouts of the bookies were now loudening outside in the sunlight, and when I'd slipped on my raincoat we went out to see what we could of the Light Weight Race.

The first two races were little more than the clamour and commotion of a passing procession. The Open Race was the main excitement of the afternoon; it was run "in colours," and there were about a dozen dashing competitors, several of them well-known winners in such events.

But everything connected with this contest reached me as though from a long way off, since I was half-stupefied by yawning nervousness. They appeared to be accomplishing something incredible by galloping round the course. I had got to do it myself in half an hour; and what was worse, Dixon was relying on me to put up a creditable performance. He even expected me to give the others "a shaking up." Stephen had ceased to be any moral support at all: in spite of his success last year he was nearly as nervous as I was, and when the field for the Open Race had filed out of the hurdle-guarded enclosure, which did duty as the paddock, he disappeared in the direction of Jerry and I was left to face the future alone.

Also, as far as I knew, my horse hadn't yet arrived, and it was with a new species of alarm that I searched for him after I had seen the race start; the paddock and its environs now looked unfriendly and forsaken.

I discovered my confederates in a quiet corner under a hayrick. They seemed a discreet and unassuming pair, but Dixon greeted me with an invigorative grin. "I kept him away from the course as long as I could," he said confidentially. "He's quiet as a sheep, but he knows what he's here for; he's staled twice since we got here." He told me that Mr. Gaffikin was about and had been looking for me. "He says our horse stands a jolly good chance with the going as good as it is."

I said there was one place, in and out of a lane, where I'd have to be careful.

We then escorted Cockbird to the paddock; by the time we were there and I'd fetched my weight-cloth, the Open Race was over and the spectators were trooping back again. Among them was Mr. Gaffikin, who hailed me companionably with "Hullo, old chap; jolly sporting of you to be having a ride!" and thereafter took complete charge of me in a most considerate manner, going with me to the weighing tent with the weight-cloth over his arm, while I, of course, carried my saddle.

The winner of the Open Race was weighing in when we arrived, and I stepped diffidently onto the machine immediately after his glorified and perspiring vacation of the seat. Mr. Gaffikin doled out a few leads for me to slip into the leather pouches on the dark blue cloth until I tipped the scale at fourteen stone. The Clerk of the Scales, an unsmiling person with a large sallow face—he was a corn merchant—verified my name on the card and handed me my number-cloth and armlet; my number was seven; under less exacting conditions I might have wondered whether it was a lucky number, but I was pushed out of the way by Pomfret. Arthur Brandwick (in a grey bowler) was at his elbow, talking nineteen to the dozen; I caught a glimpse of Stephen's serious face; Colonel Hemson was with him, behaving exactly the same as last year, except that, having already "given the boy the horse," he could no longer say that he was going to do so if he won the race.

While Dixon was putting the last testing touches to Cockbird's straps and buckles, the little colonel came across to assure me that if Jerry didn't win there was no one he'd rather see first past the judge's waggon than me. He added that he'd taken a lot of trouble in choosing the cup—"very nice goblet shape—got it from Stegman & Wilks—excellent old firm in the city." But his eye wandered away from Cockbird; his sympathies were evidently strongly implicated in Jerry, who was as unperturbed as if he were being put into a brougham to fetch someone from the station.

Near him, Nigel Croplady was fussing round his horse, with quite a crowd round him.

The terrific "Boots" Brownrigg was puffing a cigarette with apparent unconcern; his black cap was well over his eyes and both hands were plunged in the pockets of a short blue overcoat; from one of the pockets protruded a short cutting whip. His boots were perfection. Spare-built and middle-sized, he looked absolutely undefeatable; and if he had any doubts about his own abilities he concealed them well.

Stifling another yawn, I did my best to imitate his demeanour. The bookies were bawling "Two to one bar one." Cockbird, stimulated by publicity, now began to give himself the airs of a real restive race-horse, chucking his head about, flattening his ears, and capering sideways in a manner which caused the onlookers to skip hastily out of range of his heels.

"I say, that's a classy looking quad!" exclaimed a youth who appeared to have purchased the paddock. He consulted his card, and I overheard his companion, as they turned away, saying something about "his jockey looking a bit green." "We'd better back Nigel's horse. They say he'll win for a cert."

For want of anything else to do at this critical moment I asked Dixon whether he'd put Homeward's half crown on. He said, "Yes, sir; Mr. Gaffikin's man has just done it for me, and I've got a bit on for myself. *It's a good thing*; they're laying five to one about him. Mr. Stephen's horse is at two's."

Mr. Gaffikin chimed in with "Mikado's a hot favourite. *Two to one on,* all along the line!" Mikado was Croplady's horse.

Mr. Gaffikin then tied the strings of my cap in a very tight bow; a bell jangled and a stentorian voice shouted, "Now, then, gentleman, I'm going down to the post." The blue sky suddenly went white; my heart bumped; I felt dazed and breathless. Then Mr. Gaffikin's remote voice said, "Let me give you a leg up, old chap." I grabbed hold of the reins, lifted an awkward foot, and was lifted airily onto the slippery saddle; Cockbird gave one prance and then stood still; Dixon was holding him firmly by the head. Pressing my knees into the saddle, I overheard Mr. Gaffikin's ultimate advice. "Don't go in front unless you can help it; *but keep well with 'em.*" They both wished me luck and released me to my destiny.

I felt as if I'd never been on Cockbird's back before; everything around me appeared unreal and disconnected from all my previous experience. As I followed Stephen out of the paddock in a sort of equestrian trance I caught sight of his father's face, pale and fixed in its most strenuous expression; his eyes followed his son, on whose departure he was too intent to be able to take in anyone else. We filed through a gate under some trees: "Gentleman George" was standing by the gate; he stared up at me as I passed. "That's the 'oss for my money," was all that he said, but his measured tone somehow brought me to my senses, and I was able to look about me when we got down to the starting place.

But even then I was much more a passenger than a resolute rider with his wits about him to "pinch" a good start. There were seven others. I kept close to Stephen. We lined up uneasily. While the starter (on his dumpy grey cob) was instructing us to keep the red flags on the right and the white flags on the left (which we already knew) I noticed Pomfret (on a well-bred, excitable brown) and Brownrigg (Croplady's bright chestnut looking very compact) already stealing forward on the side furthest from him.

When he said "Go," I went with the others; albeit with no sense of initiative. The galloping hoofs sounded strange. But Cockbird felt strong under me and he flicked over the first fence with level and unbroken stride; he was such a big jumper and so quick over his fences that I had to pull him back after each one in order to keep level with Jerry, who was going his best pace all the way. One of the soldiers (in a tophat) was making the running with Brownrigg and Pomfret close behind him. At the awkward fifth fence (the one on a bank) Pomfret's horse jumped sideways and blundered as he landed; this caused Pomfret to address him in uncomplimentary language, and at the next obstacle (another

awkward one) he ran out to the left, taking one of
the soldiers with him. This, to my intense relief, was
the last I saw of him. I took it at a place where a
hole had been knocked in it in the previous races.
The next thing I remember was the brook, which
had seemed wide and intimidating when I was on
foot and had now attracted a small gathering of
spectators. But water jumps are deceptive things and
Cockbird shot over this one beautifully. (Stephen
had told me afterwards that he'd "never seen a horse
throw such an enormous lep.") We went on up a
long slope of firm pasture land, and I now became
aware of my responsibility; my arms were aching
and my fingers were numb and I found it increas-
ingly difficult to avoid taking the lead, for after
jumping a couple more fences and crossing a field
of light ploughland we soared over a hedge with a
big drop and began to go down the other side of the
hill. Jerry was outpaced and I was level with Mikado
and the cavalry soldier who had been cutting out
the work. As Stephen dropped behind he said, "Go
on, George; you've got 'em stone-cold."

We were now more than three parts of the way
round, and there was sharp turn left-handed where
we entered on the last half-mile of the course. I lost
several lengths here by taking a wide sweep round
the white flag, which Brownrigg almost touched
with his left boot. At the next fence the soldier went

head over heels, so it was just as well for me that I was a few lengths behind him. He and his horse were still rolling about on the ground when I landed well clear of them. Brownrigg looked round and then went steadily on across a level and rather wet field which compelled me to take my last pull at Cockbird. Getting on to better ground, I remembered Mr. Gaffikin's advice, and let my horse go after him. When I had drawn up to him it was obvious that Cockbird and Mikado were the only ones left in it. I was alone with the formidable Brownrigg. The difference between us was that he was quite self-contained and I was palpitating with excitement.

We were side by side: approaching the fourth fence from the finish he hit his horse and went ahead. This caused Cockbird to quicken his pace and make his first mistake in the race by going too fast at the fence. He hit it hard and pecked badly; Brownrigg, of course, had steadied Mikado for the jump after the quite legitimate little piece of strategy which so nearly caused me to "come unstuck." Nearly, but not quite. For after my arrival at Cockbird's ears his recovery tipped me halfway back again and he cantered on across the next field with me clinging round his neck. At one moment I was almost in front of his chest. I said to myself, " I *won't* fall off," as I gradually worked my way back into the saddle. My horse was honestly following Mikado, and my fate depended on whether I could get into the saddle before we arrived at the next fence. This I just succeeded in doing, and we got over somehow. I then regained my stirrups and set off in urgent pursuit.

After that really remarkable recovery of mine, life became lyrical, beatified, ecstatic, or anything else you care to call it. To put it tersely, I just galloped past Brownrigg, sailed over the last two fences, and won by ten lengths. Stephen came in a bad third. I also remember seeing Roger Pomfret ride up to Jaggett in the paddock and inform him in a most aggressive voice that he'd got to "something well pay up and look pleasant."

Needless to say that Dixon's was the first face I was aware of; his eager look and the way he said, "Well done," were beyond all doubt the quintessence of what my victory meant to me. All else was irrelevant at that moment, even Stephen's unselfish exultation and Mr. Gaffikin's loquacious enthusiasm. As for Cockbird, no words could ever express what we felt about him. He had become the equine equivalent of Divinity.

Excited as I was, an inward voice cautioned me to control my volubility. So when I had weighed in and returned with my saddle to find a cluster of knowing ones casting an eye over the winner, I just waited soberly until Dixon had rubbed him down, mounted, and ridden serenely out of sight. The colonel was on the spot to congratulate me on my "nailing good performance" and, better still, to give Dixon his due for having got Cockbird so fit. Those few lofty minutes when he was making so much of his horse were Dixon's reward for all the trouble he had taken since Cockbird had been in his charge. He had needed no such incentive, but he asked for nothing more. While he was on his way back to Downfield he may also have thought to himself how he had made me into a good enough rider to have got round the course without a catastrophe. (He had yet to hear full details of the race—including my peculiar acrobatics towards the end, which had been witnessed by no one except the rider of Mikado, who had been kind enough to tell Croplady that he never saw such a thing in his life, which was, I hoped, intended as a compliment).

When I had watched Dixon's departure I found that public interest was being focused on the Yeomanry Team Race. I was glad to slip away by myself. A few fields out in the country I relaxed my legs on a five-barrel gate and contemplated my achievement with as much mental detachment as I could muster. Even in those days I had an instinct for getting the full flavour of an experience. Perhaps I was fortunate in not yet having become aware that the winner of the last race is forgotten as soon as the next one starts.

Forty minutes later I had claimed my cup (there was no ceremony of presentation). Having crammed the ebony pedestal into my kit bag I came out into the paddock with the cup in my other hand. It was convenient to carry, for it had handles to it.

Good-natured Arthur Brandwick came up and offered me a lift back to Downfield. While he was patting me on the back I caught sight of a figure which seemed somehow familiar. A loose-built ruddy-faced young sportsman was talking to a couple of jovial whiskered farmers; he sat on a shooting-stick with his thin neatly gaitered legs straightened; a brown felt hat was tipped well over his blunt nose, for the five o'clock sun was glaring full in his eyes. I wondered who it was he reminded me of. Brandwick answered my unspoken question.

"D' you twig who that is?" I shook my head. "Well, take another good look at him. It's our new master, and a hell of a good lad he is, from all I've heard. Up till a month ago everyone thought the country 'd have to be hunted by a committee next season. There was something fishy about every one of the coves who'd applied for the mastership. And then this chap wrote and offered to hunt the hounds himself and put up fifteen thousand a year if we guaranteed him another two thousand. Hardly a soul knew about it till today. We're lucky to get him. He's been hunting a good rough country in Ireland the last two seasons and showing rare sport. He's run across for a couple of days to look at us." As we walked away the new master turned his head and favoured us with a slow and rather blank stare.

"What did you say his name was?" I asked, when we were out of earshot. Brandwick informed me that his name was Milden—Denis Milden—and I knew that I'd known it all the time, though I hadn't set eyes on him since I was eleven years old.

Aquamarine and celestial were the shoals of sunset as I hacked pensively home from Dumbridge. The Colonel's Cup clinked and joggled against my saddle. Time was irrelevant. But I was back at Butley by eight o'clock, and Cockbird, who had returned by an earlier train, was safe and sound; a little uneasily he wandered around his loose-box, rustling the deep straw, but always going back to the manger for another mouthful of clover hay. Dixon serenely digested triumph with his tea; presently he would go out to the "Rose and Crown" to hand Homeward his multiplied half crown and overawe the gossips with his glory.

Absolved and acquiescent was the twilight as I went quietly across the lawn and in at the garden door to the drawing room. Aunt Evelyn's armchair scrooped on the beeswaxed floor as she pushed it back and stood up with her bottle of smelling salts in her hand. For the first time since my success I really felt like a hero. And Miriam served the dinner with the tired face of a saint that seemed lit with foreknowledge of her ultimate reward. But at that time I didn't know what her goodness meant.

At the end of our evening, when they had gone upstairs with my highly coloured history of the day in their heads, I strolled out into the garden; for quite a long time I stared at the friendly lights that twinkled from the railway station and along the dark Weald. I had brought something home with me as well as the Cup. There was this new idea of Denis Milden as master. For I hadn't forgotten him, and my persistent studying of *Horse and Hound* and *The Hunting Directory* had kept me acquainted with his career as an amateur huntsman since he had left Oxford. A dog barked and a train went along the Weald . . . the last train to London, I thought. . . .

Going back to the drawing room, I lit a pair of candles which made their miniature gold reflections on the shining surface of the massive Cup. I couldn't keep my eyes away from it. I looked round the shadowed room on which all my childhood and adolescence had converged, but everything led back to the talisman; while I gazed and gazed on its luster I said to myself, aloud, "It can't be true that it's really there on the table!" The photograph of Watts's "Love and Death" was there on the wall, but it meant no more to me than the strangeness of the stars which I had seen without question, out in the quiet spring night. I was secure in a cozy little universe of my own, and it had rewarded me with the Colonel's Cup. My last thought before I fell asleep was, "Next season I'll come out in a pink coat."

Sensations of a Cavalry Charge

⟅ ❧ ⟆

[**WINSTON CHURCHILL**]

It is not my purpose in this record of personal
impressions to give a general account of the
Battle of Omdurman. The story has been told
so often and in such exact military detail that everyone who is interested in the subject is no doubt well
acquainted with what took place. I shall only sum-
marize the course of the battle so far as may be necessary to explain my own experiences.

The whole of the Khalifa's army, nearly 60,000
strong, advanced in battle order from their encampment of the night before, topped the swell of
ground which hid the two armies from one another, and then rolled down the gently sloping
amphitheatre in the arena of which, backed upon
the Nile, Kitchener's 20,000 troops were drawn up
shoulder to shoulder to receive them. Ancient and

modern confronted one another. The weapons, the methods and the fanaticism of the Middle Ages were brought by an extraordinary anachronism into dire collision with the organisation and inventions of the nineteenth century. The result was not surprising. As the successors of the Saracens descended the long smooth slopes which led to the river and their enemy, they encountered the rifle fire of two and a half divisions of trained infantry, drawn up two deep and in close order and supported by at least 70 guns on the riverbank and in the gunboats, all firing with undisturbed efficiency. Under this fire the whole attack withered and came to a standstill, with a loss of perhaps six or seven thousand men, at least 700 yards away from the British-Egyptian line. The Dervish army, however, possessed nearly 20,000 rifles of various kinds, from the most antiquated to the most modern, and when the spearmen could get no farther, these riflemen lay down on the plain and began a ragged, unaimed but considerable fusillade at the dark line of the thorn-fence zariba. Now for the first time they began to inflict losses on their antagonists, and in the short space that this lasted, perhaps two hundred casualties occurred among the British and Egyptian troops.

Seeing that the attack had been repulsed with great slaughter and that he was nearer to the city of Omdurman than the Dervish army, Kitchener immediately wheeled his five brigades into his usual echelon formation, and with his left flank on the river proceeded to march south towards the city, intending thereby to cut off what he considered to be the remnants of the Dervish army from their capital, their base, their food, their water, their home, and to drive them out into the vast deserts which stared on every side. But the Dervishes were by no means defeated. The whole of their left, having overshot the mark, had not even been under fire. The Khalifa's reserve of perhaps 15,000 men was still intact. All these swarms now advanced with undaunted courage to attack the British and Egyptian forces, which were no longer drawn up in a prepared position, but marching freely over the desert. This second shock was far more critical than the first. The charging Dervishes succeeded everywhere in coming to within a hundred or two hundred yards of the troops, and the rear brigade of Soudanese, attacked from two directions, was only saved from destruction by the skill and firmness of its commander, General Hector Macdonald. However, discipline and machinery triumphed over the most desperate valour, and after an enormous carnage, certainly exceeding 20,000 men, who strewed the ground in heaps and swathes "like snowdrifts," the whole mass of the Dervishes dissolved into fragments and into particles and streamed away into the fantastic mirages of the desert.

The Egyptian cavalry and the camel corps had been protecting the right flank of the zariba when it was attacked, and the 21st Lancers were the only horsemen on the left flank nearest to Omdurman. Immediately after the first attack had been repulsed, we were ordered to leave the zariba, ascertain what enemy forces, if any, stood between Kitchener and the city, and if possible drive these forces back and clear the way for the advancing army. Of course as a regimental officer one knows very little of what is taking place over the whole field of battle. We waited by our horses during the first attack close down by the river's edge, sheltered by the steep Nile bank from the bullets which whistled overhead. As soon as the fire began to slacken and it was said on all sides that the attack had been repulsed, a general arrived with his staff at a gallop with instant orders to mount and advance. In two minutes the four squadrons were mounted and trotting out of the zariba in a southerly direction. We ascended again the slopes of Jebel Surgham which had played its part in the first stages of the action, and from its ridges soon saw before us the whole plain of Omdurman with the vast mud city, its minarets and domes, spread before us six or seven miles away. After various halts and reconnoiterings we found ourselves walking forward in what is called "column of troops." There are four troops in a squadron and four squadrons in a regiment. Each of these troops now followed the other. I commanded the second troop from the rear, comprising between twenty and twenty-five Lancers.

Everyone expected that we were going to make a charge. That was the one idea that had been in all minds since we had started from Cairo. Of course there would be a charge. In those days, before the Boer War, British cavalry had been taught little else. Here was clearly the occasion for a charge. But against what body of enemy, over what ground, in which direction or with what purpose, were matters hidden from the rank and file. We continued to pace forward over the hard sand, peering into the mirage-twisted plain in a high state of suppressed excitement. Presently I noticed, 300 yards away on our flank and parallel to the line on which we were advancing, a long row of blue-black objects, two or three yards apart. I thought there were about a hundred and fifty. Then I became sure that these were men—enemy men—squatting on the ground. Almost at the same moment the trumpet sounded, "Trot," and the whole column of cavalry began to jingle and clatter across the front of these crouching figures. We were in the lull of the battle and there was perfect silence. Forthwith from every blue-black blob came a white puff of smoke, and a loud volley of musketry broke the odd stillness. Such a target at such a distance could scarcely be missed, and all along the column here and there horses bounded and a few men fell.

The intentions of our colonel had no doubt been to move round the flank of the body of Dervishes he had now located, and who, concealed in a fold of the ground behind their riflemen, were invisible to us, and then to attack them from a more advantageous quarter; but once the fire was opened and losses began to grow, he must have judged it inexpedient to prolong his procession across the open plain. The trumpet sounded "Right wheel into line," and all the sixteen troops swung round towards the blue-black riflemen. Almost immediately the regiment broke into a gallop, and the 21st Lancers were committed to their first charge in war!

I propose to describe exactly what happened to me; what I saw and what I felt. I recalled it to my mind so frequently after the event that the impression is as clear and vivid as it was a quarter of a century ago. The troop I commanded was, when we wheeled into line, the second from the right of the regiment. I was riding a handy, sure-footed, grey Arab polo pony. Before we wheeled and began to gallop, the officers had been marching with drawn swords. On account of my shoulder I had always decided that if I were involved in hand-to-hand fighting, I must use a pistol and not a sword. I had purchased in London a Mauser automatic pistol, then the newest and the latest design. I had practised carefully with this during our march and journey up the river. This then was the weapon with which I determined to fight. I had first of all to return my sword into its scabbard, which is not the easiest thing to do at a gallop. I had then to draw my pistol from its wooden holster and bring it to full cock. This dual operation took an appreciable time, and until it was finished, apart from a few glances to my left to see what effect the fire was producing, I did not look up at the general scene.

Then I saw immediately before me, and now only half the length of a polo ground away, the row of crouching blue figures firing frantically, wreathed in white smoke. On my right and left my neighbouring troop leaders made a good line. Immediately behind was a long dancing row of lances couched for the charge. We were going at a fast but steady gallop. There was too much trampling and rifle fire to hear any bullets. After this glance to the right and left and at my troop, I looked again towards the enemy. The scene appeared to be suddenly transformed. The blue-black men were still firing, but behind them there now came into view a depression like a shallow sunken road. This was crowded and crammed with men rising up from the ground where they had hidden. Bright flags appeared as if by magic, and I saw arriving from nowhere emirs on horseback among and around the mass of the enemy. The Dervishes appeared to be ten or twelve deep at the thickest, a great grey mass gleaming with steel, filling the dry watercourse. In the same twinkling of an eye I saw also that our right overlapped their left, that my troop would just strike the edge of their array, and that the troop on my right would charge into air. My subaltern comrade on the right, Wormald of the 7th Hussars, could see the situation too, and we both increased our speed to the very fastest gallop and curved inward like the horns of the moon. One really had not time to be frightened or to think of anything else but these particular necessary actions which I have described. They completely occupied mind and senses.

The collision was now very near. I saw immediately before me, not ten yards away, the two blue men who lay in my path. They were perhaps a couple of yards apart. I rode at the interval between them. They both fired. I passed through the smoke conscious that I was unhurt. The trooper immediately behind me was killed at this place and at this moment, whether by these shots or not I do not know. I checked my pony as the ground began to fall away beneath his feet. The clever animal dropped like a cat four or five feet down onto the sandy bed of the watercourse, and in this sandy bed

I found myself surrounded by what seemed to be dozens of men. They were not thickly packed enough at this point for me to experience any actual collision with them. Whereas Grenfell's troop, next but one on my left, was brought to a complete standstill and suffered very heavy losses, we seemed to push our way through as one has sometimes seen mounted policemen break up a crowd. In less time then it takes to relate, my pony had scrambled up the other side of the ditch. I looked round.

Once again I was on the hard, crisp desert, my horse at a trot. I had the impression of scattered Dervishes running to and fro in all directions. Straight before me a man threw himself on the ground. The reader must remember that I had been trained as a cavalry soldier to believe that if ever cavalry broke into a mass of infantry, the latter would be at their mercy. My first idea therefore was that the man was terrified. But simultaneously I saw the gleam of his curved sword as he drew it back for a ham-stringing cut. I had room and time enough to turn my pony out of his reach, and leaning over on the off side I fired two shots into him at about three yards. As I straightened myself in the saddle, I saw before me another figure with uplifted sword. I raised my pistol and fired. So close were we that the pistol itself actually struck him. Man and sword disappeared below and behind me. On my left, ten yards away, was an Arab horseman in a bright-coloured tunic and steel helmet, with chain mail hangings. I fired at him. He turned aside. I pulled my horse into a walk and looked around again.

In one respect a cavalry charge is very like ordinary life. So long as you are all right, firmly in the saddle, your horse in hand, and well armed, lots of enemies will give you a wide berth. But as soon as you have lost a stirrup, have a rein cut, have dropped your weapon, are wounded, or your horse is wounded, then is the moment when from all quarters enemies rush upon you. Such was the fate of not a few of my comrades in the troops immediately on my left. Brought to an actual standstill in the enemy's mass, clutched at from every side, stabbed at and hacked at by spear and sword, they were dragged from their horses and cut to pieces by the infuriated foe. But this I did not at the time see or understand. My impressions continued to be sanguine. I thought we were masters of the situation, riding the enemy down, scattering them and killing them. I pulled my horse up and looked about me. There was a mass of Dervishes about forty or fifty yards away on my left. They were huddling and clumping themselves together, rallying for mutual protection. They seemed wild with excitement, dancing about on their feet, shaking their spears up and down. The whole scene seemed to flicker. I have an impression, but it is too fleeting to define, of brown-clad Lancers mixed up here and there with this surging mob. The scattered individuals in my immediate neighbourhood made no attempt to molest me. Where was my troop? Where were the other troops of the squadron? Within a hundred yards of me I could not see a single officer or man. I looked back at the Dervish mass. I saw two or three riflemen crouching and aiming their rifles at me from the fringe of it. Then for the first time that morning I experienced a sudden sensation of fear. I felt myself absolutely alone. I thought those rifle-men would hit me and the rest devour me like wolves. What a fool I was to loiter like this in the midst of the enemy! I crouched over the saddle, spurred my horse into a gallop and drew clear of the *mêlée*. Two or three hundred yards away I found my troop already faced about and partly formed up.

The other three troops of the squadron were re-forming close by. Suddenly in the midst of the troop up sprang a Dervish. How he got there I do not know. He must have leaped out of some scrub or hole. All the troopers turned upon him thrusting with their lances; but he darted to and fro causing for the moment a frantic commotion. Wounded several times, he staggered towards me raising his spear. I shot him at less than a yard. He fell on the sand, and lay there dead. How easy to kill a man!

But I did not worry about it. I found I had fired the whole magazine of my Mauser pistol, so I put in a new clip of ten cartridges before thinking of anything else.

I was still prepossessed with the idea that we had inflicted great slaughter on the enemy and had scarcely suffered at all ourselves. Three or four men were missing from my troop. Six men and nine or ten horses were bleeding from spear thrusts or sword cuts. We all expected to be ordered immediately to charge back again. The men were ready, though they all looked serious. Several asked to be allowed to throw away their lances and draw their swords. I asked my second sergeant if he had enjoyed himself. His answer was, "Well, I don't exactly say I enjoyed it, sir; but I think I'll get more used to it next time." At this the whole troop laughed.

But now from the direction of the enemy there came a succession of grisly apparitions; horses spouting blood, struggling on three legs, men staggering on foot, men bleeding from terrible wounds, fish-hook spears stuck right through them, arms and faces cut to pieces, bowels protruding, men gasping, crying, collapsing, expiring. Our first task was to succour these; and meanwhile the blood of our leaders cooled. They remembered for the first time that we had carbines. Everything was still in great confusion. But trumpets were sounded and orders shouted, and we all moved off at a trot towards the flank of the enemy. Arrived at a position from which we could enfilade and rake the watercourse, two squadrons were dismounted and in a few minutes with their fire at three hundred yards compelled the Dervishes to retreat. We therefore remained in possession of the field. Within twenty minutes of the time when we had first wheeled into line and began our charge, we were halted and breakfasting in the very watercourse that had so nearly proved our undoing. There one could see the futility of the much vaunted *Arme Blanche*. The Dervishes had carried off their wounded, and the corpses of thirty or forty enemies were all that could be counted on the ground. Among these lay the bodies of over twenty Lancers, so hacked and mutilated as to be mostly unrecognisable. In all, out of 310 officers and men, the regiment had lost in the space of about two or three minutes five officers and sixty-five men killed and wounded, and 120 horses—nearly a quarter of its strength.

Such were my fortunes in this celebrated episode. It is very rarely that cavalry and infantry, while still both unshaken, are intermingled as the result of an actual collision. Either the infantry keep their heads and shoot the cavalry down, or they break into confusion and are cut down or speared as they run. But the two or three thousand Dervishes who faced the

21st Lancers in the watercourse at Omdurman were not in the least shaken by the stress of battle or afraid of cavalry. Their fire was not good enough to stop the charge, but they had no doubt faced horsemen many a time in the wars with Abyssinia. They were familiar with the ordeal of the charge. It was the kind of fighting they thoroughly understood. Moreover, the fight was with equal weapons, for the British, too, fought with sword and lance as in the days of old.

"Philippa's Fox-Hunt" from Some Experiences of an Irish R.M.

[E. OE SOMERVILLE AND MARTIN ROSS]

No one can accuse Philippa and me of having married in haste. As a matter of fact, it was but little under five years from that autumn evening on the river when I had said what is called in Ireland "the hard word," to the day in August when I was led to the altar by my best man, and was subsequently led away from it by Mrs. Sinclair Yeates. About two years out of the five had been spent by me at Shreelane in ceaseless warfare with drains, eaveshoots, chimneys, pumps; all those fundamentals, in short, that the ingenuous and improving tenant expects to find established as a basis from which to rise to higher things. As far as rising to higher things went, frequent ascents to the roof to search for leaks summed up my achievements; in fact, I suffered so general a shrinkage of my ideals that the triumph of making the hall-door bell ring blinded me to the fact that the rat holes in the hall floor were nailed up with pieces of tin biscuit boxes, and that the casual visitor could, instead of leaving a card, have easily written his name in the damp on the walls.

Philippa, however, proved adorably callous to these and similar shortcomings. She regarded Shreelane and its floundering, foundering ménage of incapables in the light of a gigantic picnic in a foreign land. She held long conversations daily with Mrs. Cadogan, in order, as she informed me, to acquire the language. Without any ulterior domestic intention she engaged kitchen maids because of the beauty of their eyes, and house-maids because they had such delightfully picturesque old mothers, and she declined to correct the phraseology of the parlor maid, whose painful habit it was to whisper "Do ye choose cherry or clarry?" when proffering the wine. Fast days, perhaps, afforded my wife her first insight into the sterner realities of Irish house-keeping. Philippa had what are known as High Church proclivities, and took the matter seriously.

"I don't know how we are to manage for the servants' dinner tomorrow, Sinclair," she said, coming into my office on Thursday morning. "Julia says she 'promised God this long time that she wouldn't eat an egg on a fast day,' and the kitchen maid says she won't eat herrings 'without they're fried with onions,' and Mrs. Cadogan says she will 'not go to them extremes for servants.' "

"I should let Mrs. Cadogen settle the menu herself," I suggested.

"I asked her to do that," replied Philippa, "and she only said she 'thanked God *she* had no appetite!' "

The lady of the house here fell away into unseasonable laughter.

I made the demoralising suggestion that, as we were going away for a couple of nights, we might safely leave them to fight it out, and the problem was abandoned.

Philippa had been much called on by the neighbourhood in all its shades and grades, and daily she and her trousseau frocks presented themselves at hall doors of varying dimensions in due acknowledgement of civilities. In Ireland, it may be noted, the process known in England as "summering and wintering" a newcomer does not obtain—sociability and curiosity alike forbid delay. The visit to which we owed our escape from the intricacies of the fast day was to the Knoxes of Castle Knox, relations in some remote and tribal way of my landlord, Mr. Flurry, of that ilk. It involved a short journey by train, and my wife's longest basket trunk. It also, which was more serious, involved my being lent a horse to go out cubbing the following morning.

At Castle Knox we sank into an almost forgotten environment of draught-proof windows and doors, of deep carpets, of silent servants instead of clattering belligerents. Philippa told me afterwards that it had only been by an effort that she had restrained herself from snatching up the train of her wedding gown as she paced across the wide hall on little Sir Valentine's arm. After three weeks at Shreelane she found it difficult to remember that the floor was neither damp nor dusty.

I had the good fortune to be of the limited number of those who got on with Lady Knox, chiefly, I imagine, because I was as a worm before her, and thankfully permitted her to do all the talking.

"Your wife is extremely pretty," she pronounced autocratically, surveying Philippa between the candle shades. "Does she ride?"

Lady Knox was a short square lady, with a weather-beaten face, and an eye decisive from long habit of taking her own line across country and elsewhere. She would have made a very imposing little coachman, and would have caused her stable helpers to rue the day they had the presumption to be born. It struck me that Sir Valentine sometimes did so.

"I'm glad you like her looks," I replied, "as I fear you will find her thoroughly despicable otherwise. For one thing, she not only can't ride, but she believes that I can!"

"Oh come, you're not as bad as all that!" my hostess was good enough to say. "I'm going to put you up on Sorcerer tomorrow, and we'll see you at the top of the hunt—if there is one. That young Knox hasn't a notion how to draw these woods."

"Well, the best run we had last year out of this place was with Flurry's hounds," struck in Miss Sally, sole daughter of Sir Valentine's house and home, from her place halfway down the table. It was not difficult to see that she and her mother held different views on the subject of Mr. Flurry Knox.

"I call it a criminal thing in anyone's great-great-grandfather to rear up a preposterous troop of sons and plant them all out in his own country," Lady Knox said to me with apparent irrelevance. "I detest collaterals. Blood may be thicker than water, but it is also a great deal nastier. In this country I find that fifteenth cousins consider themselves near relations if they live within twenty miles of one!"

Having before now taken in the position with regard to Flurry Knox, I took care to accept these remarks as generalities, and turned the conversation to other themes.

"I see Mrs. Yeates is doing wonders with Mr. Hamilton," said Lady Knox presently, following the direction of my eyes, which had strayed to where Philippa was beaming upon her left-hand neighbour, a mildewed-looking old clergyman, who was delivering a long dissertation, the purport of which we were happily unable to catch.

"She has always had a gift for the Church," I said.

"Not curates?" said Lady Knox, in her deep voice.

I made haste to reply that it was the elders of the Church who were venerated by my wife.

"Well, she has her fancy in old Eustace Hamilton. He's elderly enough!" said Lady Knox. "I wonder if she'd venerate him as much if she knew that he had fought with his sister-in-law, and they haven't spoken for thirty years! Though for the matter of that," she added, "I think it shows his good sense!"

"Mrs. Knox is rather a friend of mine," I ventured.

"Is she? H'm! Well, she's not one of mine!" replied my hostess, with her usual definiteness. "I'll say one thing for her, I believe she's always been a sportswoman. She's very rich, you know, and they say she only married old Badger Knox to save his hounds from being sold to pay his debts, and then she took the horn from him and hunted them herself. Has she been rude to your wife yet? No? Oh, well, she will. It's a mere question of time. She hates all English people. You know the story they tell of her? She was coming home from London, and when she was getting her ticket the man asked if she had a ticket for York. 'No, thank God, Cork!' says Mrs. Knox."

"Well, I rather agree with her!" said I. "But why did she fight with Mr. Hamilton?"

"Oh, nobody knows. I don't believe they know themselves! Whatever it was, the old lady drives five miles to Fortwilliam every Sunday, rather than go to his church, just outside her own back gates," Lady Knox said with a laugh like a terrier's bark. "I wish I'd fought with him myself," she said; "he gives us forty minutes every Sunday."

As I struggled into my boots the following morning, I felt that Sir Valentine's acid confidences on cub-hunting, bestowed on me at midnight, did credit to his judgment. "A very moderate amusement, my dear Major," he had said, in his dry little voice. "You should stick to shooting. No one expects you to shoot before daybreak."

It was six o'clock as I crept downstairs, and found Lady Knox and Miss Sally at breakfast, with two lamps on the table, and a foggy daylight oozing in from under the half-raised blinds. Phlippa was already in the hall, pumping up her bicycle, in a state of excitement at the prospect of her first experience at hunting that would have been more comprehensible to me had she been going to ride a strange horse, as I was. As I bolted my food I saw the horses being led past the windows, and a faint twang of a horn told that Flurry Knox and his hounds were not far off.

Miss Sally jumped up.

"If I'm not on the Cockatoo before the hounds come up, I shall never get there!" she said, hobbling out of the room in the toils of her safety habit. Her small, alert face looked very childish under her riding hat; the lamp light struck sparks out of her thick coil of golden-red hair; I wondered how I had ever thought her like her prim little father.

She was already on her white cob when I got to the hall door, and Flurry Knox was riding over the glistening wet grass with his hounds, while his whip, Dr. Jerome Hickey, was having a stirring time with the young entry and the rabbit holes. They moved on without stopping, up a back avenue under tall and dripping trees, to a thick laurel covert, at some little distance from the house. Into this the hounds were thrown, and the usual period of fidgety inaction set in for the riders, of whom, all told, there were about half a dozen. Lady Knox, square and solid on her big, confidential iron-grey, was near me, and her eyes were on me and my mount. With her rubicund face and white collar she was more than ever like a coachman.

"Sorcerer looks as if he suited you well," she said, after a few minutes of silence, during which the hounds rustled and crackled steadily through the laurels. "He's a little high on the leg, and so are you, you know, so you show each other off."

Sorcerer was standing like a rock, with his good-looking head in the air and his eyes fastened on the covert. His manners, so far, had been those of a perfect gentleman, and were in marked contrast to those of Miss Sally's cob, who was sidling, hopping, and snatching unappeasably at his bit. Philippa had disappeared from view down the avenue ahead. The fog was melting, and the sun threw long blades of light through the trees. Everything was quiet, and in the distance the curtained windows of the house marked the warm repose of Sir Valentine, and those of the party who shared his opinion of cubbing.

"Hark! Hark to cry there!"

It was Flurry's voice, away at the other side of the covert. The rustling and brushing through the laurels became more vehement, then passed out of hearing.

"He never will leave his hounds alone," said Lady Knox disapprovingly.

Miss Sally and the Cockatoo moved away in a series of heraldic capers towards the end of the laurel plantation, and at the same moment I saw Philippa on her bicycle shoot into view on the drive ahead of us.

"I've seen a fox!" she screamed, white with what I believe to have been personal terror, though she says it was excitement. "It passed quite close to me!"

"What way did he go?" bellowed a voice which I recognised as Dr. Hickey's, somewhere in the deep of the laurels.

"Down the drive!" returned Philippa, with a pea-hen quality in her tones with which I was quite unacquainted.

An electrifying screech of "Gone away!" was projected from the laurels by Dr. Hickey.

"Gone away!" chanted Flurry's horn at the top of the covert.

"This is what he calls cubbing!" said Lady Knox. "A mere farce!" But nonetheless she loosed her sedate monster into a canter.

Sorcerer got his hind legs under him, and hardened his crest against the bit, as we all hustled along the drive after the flying figure of my wife. I knew very little about horses, but I realised that even with the hounds tumbling hysterically out of the covert, and the Cockatoo kicking the gravel into his face, Sorcerer comported himself with the manners of the best society. Up a side road I saw Flurry Knox opening half of a gate and cramming through it; in a moment we also had crammed through, and the turf of a pasture field was under our feet. Dr. Hickey leaned forward and took hold of his horse. I did likewise, with the trifling difference that my horse took hold of me, and I steered for Flurry Knox with single-hearted purpose, the hounds, already a field ahead, being merely an exciting and noisy accompaniment of this endeavour. A heavy stone wall was the first occurrence of note. Flurry chose a place where the top was loose, and his clumsy-looking brown mare changed feet on the rattling stones like a fairy. Sorcerer came at it, tense

and collected as a bow at full stretch, and sailed
steeply into the air. I saw the wall far beneath me,
with an unsuspected ditch on the far side, and I felt
my hat following me at the full stretch of its guard
as we swept over it, then, with a long slant, we descended to earth some sixteen feet from where we
had left it and I was possessor of the gratifying fact
that I had achieved a good-sized "fly," and had
not perceptibly moved in my saddle. Subsequent
disillusioning experience has taught me that but
few horses jump like Sorcerer, so gallantly, so sym-
pathetically, and with such supreme mastery of the
subject. But nonetheless the enthusiasm that he im-
parted to me has never been extinguished, and that
October morning ride revealed to me the unsuspected intoxication of fox-hunting.

Behind me I heard the scrabbling of the Cockatoo's little hoofs among the loose stones, and Lady
Knox, galloping on my left, jerked a maternal chin
over her shoulder to mark her daughter's progress.
For my part, had there been an entire circus behind
me, I was far too much occupied with ramming on
my hat and trying to hold Sorcerer, to have looked
round, and all my spare faculties were devoted to
steering for Flurry, who had taken a right-handed
turn, and was at that moment surmounting a bank
of uncertain and briary aspect. I surmounted it also,
with the swiftness and simplicity for which the

Quaker's methods of bank jumping had not prepared me, and two or three fields, traversed at the
same steeplechase pace, brought us to a road and to
a abrupt check. There, suddenly, were the hounds,
scrambling in baffled silence down into the road
from the opposite bank, to look for the line they
had overrun, and there, amazingly, was Philippa, engaged in excited converse with several men with
spades over their shoulders.

"Did ye see the fox, boys?" shouted Flurry, addressing the group.

"We did! We did!" cried my wife and her friends
in chorus. "He ran up the road!"

"We'd be badly off without Mrs. Yeates!" said
Flurry, as he whirled his mare round and clattered
up the road with a hustle of hounds after him.

It occurred to me as forcibly as any mere earthly
thing can occur to those who are wrapped in the
sublimities of a run that, for a young woman who
had never before seen a fox out of a cage at the zoo,
Philippa was taking to hunting very kindly. Her
cheeks were a most brilliant pink, her blue eyes
shone.

"Oh, Sinclair!" she exclaimed, "they say he's going
for Aussolas, and there's a road I can ride all the
way!"

"Ye can, Miss! Sure we'll show you!" chorused
her *cortège*.

Her foot was on the pedal ready to mount. Decidedly my wife was in no need of assistance from me.

Up the road a hound gave a yelp of discovery and flung himself over a stile into the fields. The rest of the pack went squealing and jostling after him, and I followed Flurry over one of those infinitely varied erections, pleasantly termed "gaps" in Ireland. On this occasion the gap was made of three razor-edged slabs of slate leaning against an iron bar, and Sorcerer conveyed to me his thorough knowledge of the matter by a lift of his hindquarters that made me feel as if I were being skillfully kicked downstairs. To what extent I looked it, I cannot say, nor providentially can Philippa, as she had already started. I only know that undeserved good luck restored to me my stirrup before Sorcerer got away with me in the next field.

What followed was, I am told, a very fast fifteen minutes. For me time was not: the empty fields rushed past uncounted, fences came and went in a flash, while the wind sang in my ears, and the dazzle of the early sun was in my eyes. I saw the hounds occasionally, sometimes pouring over a green bank, as the charging breaker lifts and flings itself, sometimes driving across a field, as the white tongues of foam slide racing over the sand; and always ahead of me was Flurry Knox, going as a man goes who knows his country, who knows his horse, and whose heart is wholly and absolutely in the right place.

Do what I could, Sorcerer's implacable stride carried me closer and closer to the brown mare, till, as I thundered down the slope of a long field, I was not twenty yards behind Flurry. Sorcerer had stiffened his neck to iron, and to slow him down was beyond me, but I fought his head away to the right, and found myself coming hard and steady at a stone-faced bank with broken ground in front of it. Flurry bore away to the left, shouting something that I did not understand. That Sorcerer shortened his stride at the right moment was entirely due to his own judgment. Standing well away from the jump, he rose like a stag out of the tussocky ground, and as he swung my twelve stone six into the air the obstacle revealed itself to him and me as consisting not of one bank but of two, and between the two lay a deep grassy lane, half choked with furze. I have often been asked to state the width of the bohereen, and can only reply that in my opinion it was at least eighteen feet; Flurry Knox and Dr. Hickey, who did not jump it, say that it was not more than five. What Sorcerer did with it I cannot say: the sensation was of a towering flight with a kickback in it, a biggish drop, and a landing on cee-springs, still on the downhill grade. That was how one of the best horses in Ireland took one of Ireland's most ignorant riders over a very nasty place.

A somber line of fir wood lay ahead, rimmed with a grey wall, and in another couple of minutes we had pulled up on the Aussolas road, and were watching the hounds struggling over the wall into Aussolas demesne.

"No hurry now," said Flurry, turning in his saddle to watch the Cockatoo jump into the road. "He's to ground in the big earth inside. Well, Major, it's well for you that's a big-jumped horse. I thought you were a dead man a while ago when you faced him at the bohereen!"

I was disclaiming intention in the matter when Lady Knox and the others joined us.

"I thought you told me your wife was no sports-woman," she said to me, critically scanning Sor-cerer's legs for cuts the while, "but when I saw her a minute ago she had abandoned her bicycle and was running across country like—"

"Look at her now!" interrupted Miss Sally. "Oh!—Oh!" In the interval between these excla-mations my incredulous eyes beheld my wife in mid-air, hand in hand with a couple of stalwart country boys, with whom she was leaping in unison from the top of a bank onto the road.

Everyone, even the saturnine Dr. Hickey, began to laugh; I rode back to Philippa, who was exchanging compliments and congratulations with her escorts.

"Oh, Sinclair!" she cried, "wasn't it splendid? I saw you jumping, and everything! Where are they going now?'

"My dear girl," I said, with marital disapproval, "you're killing yourself. Where's your bicycle?"

"Oh, it's punctured in a sort of lane, back there. It's all right; and then they"—she breathlessly waved her hand at her attendants—"they showed me the way."

"Begor! You proved very good, Miss!" said a grinning cavalier.

"Faith she did!" said another, polishing his shining brow with his white flannel coat sleeve, "she lepped like a haarse!"

"And may I ask how you propose to go home?" said I.

"I don't know and I don't care! I'm not going home!" She cast an entirely disobedient eye at me. "And your eyeglass is hanging down your back and your tie is bulging out over your waistcoat!"

The little group of riders had begun to move away.

"We're going on into Aussolas," called out Flurry. "Come on, and make my grandmother give you some breakfast, Mrs. Yeates; she always has it at eight o'clock."

The front gates were close at hand, and we turned in under the tall beech trees, with the unswept leaves rustling round the horses' feet, and the lovely blue of the October morning sky filling the spaces between smooth grey branches and

golden leaves. The woods rang with the voices of
the hounds, enjoying an untrammeled rabbit hunt,
while the master and the whip, both on foot,
strolled along unconcernedly with their bridles
over their arms, making themselves agreeable to my
wife, an occasional touch of Flurry's horn or a
crack of Dr. Hickey's whip just indicating to the
pack that the authorities still took a friendly interest in their doings.

Down a grassy glade in the wood a party of old
Mrs. Knox's young horses suddenly swept into view,
headed by an old mare who, with her tail over her
back, stampeded ponderously past our cavalcade,
shaking and swinging her handsome old head, while
her youthful friends bucked and kicked and snapped
at each other round her with the ferocious humor
of their kind.

"Here, Jerome, take the horn," said Flurry to Dr.
Hickey. "I'm going to see Mrs. Yeates up to the
house, the way these tomfools won't gallop on top
of her."

From this point it seems to me that Philippa's ad-
ventures are more worthy of record than mine, and
as she has favoured me with a full account of them,
I venture to think my version may be relied on.

Mrs. Knox was already at breakfast when Philippa
was led, quaking, into her formidable presence. My
wife's acquaintance with Mrs. Knox was, so far, lim-

ited to a state visit on either side, and she found but little comfort in Flurry's assurances that his grandmother wouldn't mind if he brought all the hounds in to breakfast, coupled with the statement that she would put her eyes on sticks for the Major.

Whatever the truth of this may have been, Mrs. Knox received her guest with an equanimity quite unshaken by the fact that her boots were in the fender instead of on her feet, and that a couple of shawls of varying dimensions and degrees of age did not conceal the inner presence of a magenta flannel dressing jacket. She installed Philippa at the table and plied her with food, oblivious as to whether the needful implements with which to eat it were forthcoming or not. She told Flurry where a vixen had reared her family, and she watched him ride away, with some biting comments on his mare's hocks screamed after him from the window.

The dining room at Aussolas Castle is one of the many rooms in Ireland in which Cromwell is said to have stabled his horse (and probably no one would have objected less than Mrs. Knox had she been consulted in the matter). Philippa questions if the room had ever been tidied up since, and she endorses Flurry's observation that "there wasn't a day in the year you wouldn't get feeding for a hen and chickens on the floor." Opposite to Philippa, on a *Louis Quinze* chair, sat Mrs. Knox's woolly dog, its

suspicious little eyes peering at her out of their setting of pink lids and dirty white wool. A couple of
young horses outside the windows tore at the mat-
ted creepers on the walls, or thrust faces that were
half-shy, half-impudent, into the room. Portly pi-
geons waddled to and fro on the broad windowsill,
sometimes flying in to perch on the picture frames,
while they kept up incessantly a hoarse and
pompous cooing.

Animals and children are, as a rule, alike destruc-
tive to conversation; but Mrs. Knox, when she
chose, *bien entendu,* could have made herself agreeable in a Noah's ark, and Philippa has a gift of sympathetic attention that personal experience has
taught me to regard with distrust as well as respect,
while it has often made me realise the worldly wis-
dom of Kingsley's injunction: "Be good, sweet maid,
and let who will be clever."

Family prayers, declaimed by Mrs. Knox with
alarming austerity, followed close on breakfast,
Philippa and a vinegar-faced henchwoman forming
the family. The prayers were long, and through the
open window as they progressed came distantly a
whoop or two; the declamatory tones staggered a
little, and then continued at a distinctly higher rate
of speed.

"Ma'am! Ma'am!" whispered a small voice at the
window.

Mrs. Knox made a repressive gesture and held on her way. A sudden outcry of hounds followed, and the owner of the whisper, a small boy with a face freckled like a turkey's egg, darted from the window and dragged a donkey and bath-chair into view. Philippa admits to having lost the thread of the discourse, but she thinks that the "amen" that immediately ensued can hardly have come in its usual place. Mrs. Knox shut the book abruptly, scrambled up from her knees, and said, "They've found!"

In a surprisingly short space of time she had added to her attire her boots, a fur cape, and a garden hat, and was in the bath-chair, the small boy stimulating the donkey with the success peculiar to his class, while Philippa hung on behind.

The woods of Aussolas are hilly and extensive, and on that particular morning it seemed that they held as many foxes as hounds. In vain was the horn blown and the whips cracked. Small rejoicing parties of hounds, each with a fox of its own, scoured to and fro. Every labourer in the vicinity had left his work, and was sedulously heading every fox with yells that would have benefited a tiger hunt, and sticks and stones when occasion served.

"Will I pull out as far as the big rosy dandhrum, ma'am" inquired the small boy. "I seen three of the dogs go in it, and they yowling."

"You will," said Mrs. Knox, thumping the donkey on the back with her umbrella. "Here! Jeremiah Regan! Come down out of that with that pitchfork! Do you want to kill the fox, you fool?"

"I do not, your honour, ma'am," responded Jeremiah Regan, a tall young countryman, emerging from a bramble brake.

"Did you see him?" said Mrs. Knox eagerly.

"I seen himself and his ten pups drinking below at the lake ere yesterday, your honour, ma'am, and he as big as a chestnut horse!" said Jeremiah.

"Faugh! Yesterday! Snorted Mrs. Knox. "Go on to the rhododendrons, Johnny!"

The party, reinforced by Jeremiah and the pitchfork, progressed at a high rate of speed along the shrubbery path, encountering en route Lady Knox, stooping onto her horse's neck under the sweeping branches of the laurels.

"Your horse is too high for my coverts, Lady Knox," said the Lady of the Manor, with a malicious eye at Lady Knox's flushed face and dinged hat. "I'm afraid you will be left behind like Absalom when the hounds go away!"

"As they never do anything here but hunt rabbits," retorted her ladyship, "I don't think that's likely."

Mrs. Knox gave her donkey another whack, and passed on.

"Rabbits, my dear!" she said scornfully to Philippa. "That's all she knows about it. I declare it disgusts me to see a woman of that age making such a Judy of herself! Rabbits indeed!"

Down in the thicket of rhododendron everything was very quiet for a time. Philippa strained her eyes in vain to see any of the riders; the horn blowing and the whip cracking passed on almost out of hearing. Once or twice a hound worked through the rhododendrons, glanced at the party, and hurried on, immersed in business. All at once Johnny, the donkey-boy, whispered excitedly:

"Look at he! Look at he!" and pointed to a boulder of grey rock that stood out among the dark evergreens. A big yellow cub was crouching on it; he instantly slid into the shelter of the bushes, and the irrepressible Jeremiah, uttering a rending shriek, plunged into the thicket after him. Two or three hounds came rushing at the sound, and after this Philippa says she finds some difficulty in recalling the proper order of events—chiefly, she confesses, because of the wholly ridiculous tears of excitement that blurred her eyes.

"We ran," she said, "we simply tore, and the donkey galloped, and as for that old Mrs. Knox, she was giving cracked screams to the hounds all the time, and they were screaming too; and then somehow we were all out on the road!"

What seems to have occurred was that three couple of hounds, Jeremiah Regan, and Mrs. Knox's equipage, amongst them somehow hustled the cub out of Aussolas demesne and up onto a hill on the farther side of the road. Jeremiah was sent back by his mistress to fetch Flurry, and the rest of the party pursued a thrilling course along the road, parallel with that of the hounds, who were hunting slowly through the gorse on the hillside.

"Upon my honour and word, Mrs. Yeates, my dear, we have the hunt to ourselves!" said Mrs. Knox to the panting Philippa, as they pounded along the road. "Johnny, d'ye see the fox?"

"I do, ma'am!" shrieked Johnny, who possessed the usual field-glass vision bestowed upon his kind. "Look at him over-right us on the hill above! Hi! The spotty dog have him! No, he's gone from him! *Gwan out o' that!*" This to the donkey, with blows that sounded like the beating of carpets, and produced rather more dust.

They had left Aussolas some half a mile behind, when, from a strip of wood on their right, the fox suddenly slipped over the bank onto the road just ahead of them, ran up it for a few yards and whisked in at a small entrance gate, with the three couple of hounds yelling on a red-hot scent, not thirty yards behind. The bath-chair party whirled in at their heels, Philippa and the donkey considerably blown,

Johnny scarlet through his freckles, but as fresh as paint, the old lady blind and deaf to all things save the chase. The hounds went raging through the shrubs beside the drive, and away down a grassy slope towards a shallow glen, in the bottom of which ran a little stream, and after them over the grass bumped the bath-chair. At the stream they turned sharply and ran up the glen towards the avenue, which crossed it by means of a rough stone viaduct.

" 'Pon me conscience, he's into the old culvert!" exclaimed Mrs. Knox. "There was one of my hounds choked there once, long ago! Beat on the donkey, Johnny!"

At this juncture, Philippa's narrative again becomes incoherent, not to say breathless. She is, however, positive that it was somewhere about here that the upset of the bath-chair occurred, but she cannot be clear as to whether she picked up the donkey or Mrs. Knox, or whether she herself was picked up by Johnny, while Mrs. Knox picked up the donkey. From my knowledge of Mrs. Knox I should say she picked up herself and no one else. At all events, the next salient point is the palpitating moment when Mrs. Knox, Johnny, and Philippa successively applying an eye to the opening of the culvert by which the stream trickled under the viaduct, while five dripping hounds bayed and leaped around them, discovered by more senses than that of sight that the fox was in it, and furthermore that one of the hounds was in it too.

"There's a sthrong grating before him at the far end," said Johnny, his head in at the mouth of the hole, his voice sounding as if he were talking into a jug, "the two of them's fighting in it; they'll be choked surely!"

"Then don't' stand gabbling there, you little fool, but get in and pull the hound out!" exclaimed Mrs. Knox, who was balancing herself on a stone in the stream.

"I'd be in dread, ma'am," whined Johnny.

"Balderdash!" said the implacable Mrs. Knox. "In with you!"

I understand that Philippa assisted Johnny into the culvert, and presume that it was in so doing that she acquired the two Robinson Crusoe bare footprints which decorated her jacket when I next met her.

"Have you got hold of him yet, Johnny?" cried Mrs. Knox up the culvert.

"I have, ma'am, by the tail," responded Johnny's voice, sepulchral in the depths.

"Can you stir him, Johnny?"

"I cannot, ma'am, and the wather is rising in it."

"Well, please God, they'll not open the mill dam!" remarked Mrs. Knox philosophically to Philippa, as she caught hold of Johnny's dirty ankles. "Hold on to the tail, Johnny!"

She hauled, with, as might be expected, no appreciable result. "Run, my dear, and look for somebody, and we'll have that fox yet!"

Philippa ran, whither she knew not, pursued by fearful visions of bursting mill dams, and maddened foxes at bay. As she sped up the avenue she heard voices, robust male voices, in a shrubbery, and made for them. Advancing along an embowered walk towards her was what she took for one wild instant to be a funeral. A second glance showed her that it was a party of clergymen of all ages, walking by twos and threes in the dappled shade of the overarching trees. Obviously she had intruded her sacrilegious presence into a clerical meeting. She acknowledges that at this awe-inspiring spectacle she faltered, but the thought of Johnny, the hound, and the fox, suffocating, possibly drowning together in the culvert, nerved her. She does not remember what she said or how she said it, but I fancy she must have conveyed to them the impression that old Mrs. Knox was being drowned, as she immediately found herself heading a charge of the Irish Church towards the scene of disaster.

Fate has not always done me well, but on this occasion it was rightfully decreed that I and the other members of the hunt should be privileged to arrive in time to see my wife and her rescue party precipitating themselves down the glen.

"Holy Biddy!" ejaculated Flurry, "is she running a paper-chase with all the parsons? But look! For pity's sake will you look at my grandmother and my Uncle Eustace?"

Mrs. Knox and her sworn enemy the old clergyman, whom I had met at dinner the night before, were standing, apparently in the stream, tugging at two bare legs that projected from a hole in the viaduct, and arguing at the top of their voices. The bath-chair lay on its side with the donkey grazing beside it, on the bank a stout archdeacon was tendering advice, and the hounds danced and howled round the entire group.

"I tell you, Eliza, you had better let the archdeacon try," thundered Mr. Hamilton.

"Then I tell you I will not!" vociferated Mrs. Knox, with a tug at the end of the sentence that elicited a subterranean lament from Johnny. "Now who was right about the second grating? I told you so twenty years ago!"

Exactly as Philippa and her rescue party arrived, the efforts of Mrs. Knox and her brother-in-law triumphed. The struggling, sopping form of Johnny was slowly drawn from the hole, drenched, speechless, but clinging to the stern of a hound, who, in its turn, had its jaws fast in the hindquarters of a limp, yellow cub.

"Oh, it's dead!" wailed Philippa, "I *did* think I should have been in time to save it!"

"Well, if that doesn't beat all!" said Dr. Hickey.

The Chimaera

[NATHANIEL HAWTHORNE]

Once, in the old, old times (for all the strange things which I tell you about happened long before anybody can remember), a fountain gushed out of a hillside, in the marvelous land of Greece. And, for aught I know, after so many thousand years, it is still gushing out of the very self-same spot. At any rate, there was the pleasant fountain, welling freshly forth and sparkling adown the hillside, in the golden sunset, when a handsome young man named Bellerophon drew near its margin. In his hand he held a bridle studded with brilliant gems, and adorned with a golden bit. Seeing an old man, and an-other of middle age, and a little boy, near the fountain, and likewise a maiden, who was dipping up some of the water in a pitcher, he paused, and begged that he might refresh himself with a draught.

"This is very delicious water," he said to the maiden as he rinsed and filled her pitcher, after drinking out of it. "Will you be kind enough to tell me whether the fountain has a name?"

"Yes, it is called the Fountain of Pirene," answered the maiden; and then she added, "My grandmother has told me that this clear fountain was once a beautiful woman, and when her son was killed by the arrow of the huntress Diana, she melted all away into tears. And so the water, which you find so cool and sweet, is the sorrow of that poor mother's heart!"

"I should not have dreamed," observed the young stranger, "that so clear a wellspring, with its gush and gurgle, and its cheery dance out of the shade into the sunlight, had so much as one teardrop in its bosom! And this, then, is Pirene! I thank you, pretty maiden, for telling me its name. I have come from a faraway country to find this very spot."

A middle-aged country fellow (he had driven his cow to drink out of the spring) stared hard at young Bellerophon, and at the handsome bridle which he carried in his hand.

"The watercourses must be getting low, friend, in your part of the world," remarked he, "if you come so far only to find the Fountain of Pirene. But, pray, have you lost a horse? I see you carry the bridle in your hand; and a pretty one it is, with that double row of bright stones upon it. If the horse was as fine as the bridle, you are much to be pitied for losing him."

"I have lost no horse," said Bellerophon, with a smile. "But I happen to be seeking a very famous one, which, as wise people have informed me, must be found hereabouts, if anywhere. Do you know whether the winged horse Pegasus still haunts the Fountain of Pirene, as he used to do in your forefathers' day?"

But then the country fellow laughed.

Some of you, my little friends, have probably heard that this Pegasus was a snow-white steed, with beautiful silvery wings, who spent most of his time on the summit of Mount Helicon. He was as wild, and as swift, and as buoyant, in his flight through the air, as any eagle that ever soared into the clouds. There was nothing else like him in the world. He had no mate; he had never been backed or bridled by a master; and for many a long year, he led a solitary and happy life.

Oh, how fine a thing it is to be a winged horse! Sleeping at night, as he did, on a lofty mountaintop, and passing the greater part of the day in the air, Pegasus seemed hardly to be a creature of the earth. Whenever he was seen, up very high above people's heads, with the sunshine on his silvery wings, you would have thought that he belonged to the sky, and that, skimming a little too low, he had got astray among our mists and vapors, and was seeking his way back again. It was very pretty to behold him to plunge into the fleecy bosom of a bright cloud, and be lost in it for a moment or two, and then break forth from the other side. Or, in a sullen rainstorm, when there was a grey pavement of clouds over the whole sky, it would sometimes happen that the winged horse descended right through it, and the glad light of the upper region would gleam after him. In another instant, it is true, both Pegasus and the pleasant light would be gone away together. But anyone who was fortunate enough to see this wondrous spectacle felt cheerful the whole day afterwards, and as much longer as the storm lasted.

In the summertime, and in the beautifullest of weather, Pegasus often alighted on the solid earth, and, closing his silvery wings, would gallop over hill and dale for pastime, as fleetly as the wind. Oftener than in any other place, he had been seen near the Fountain of Pirene, drinking the delicious water, or rolling himself upon the soft grass of the margin. Sometimes, too (but Pegasus was very dainty in his food), he would crop a few of the clover blossoms that happened to be the sweetest.

To the Fountain of Pirene, therefore, people's great-grandfathers had been in the habit of going (as long as they were youthful, and retained their faith in winged horses), in hopes of getting a glimpse at the beautiful Pegasus. But, of late years, he had been very seldom seen. Indeed, there were many of the country folks, dwelling within half an hour's walk of the fountain, who had never beheld Pegasus, and did not believe that there was any such creature in existence. The country fellow to whom Bellerophon was speaking chanced to be one of those incredulous persons.

And that was the reason he laughed.

"Pegasus indeed!" cried he, turning up his nose as high as such a flat nose could be turned up, "Pegasus, indeed! A winged horse, truly! Why, friend, are you in your senses? Of what use would wings be to a horse? Could he drag the plough so well, think you? To be sure, there might be a little saving in the expense of shoes, but then, how would a man like to see his horse flying out of the stable window?— Yes, or whisking him above the clouds, when he only wanted to ride to mill? No, no! I don't believe in Pegasus. There never was such a ridiculous kind of horse-fowl made!"

"I have some reason to think otherwise," said Bellerophon, quietly.

And then he turned to the old, grey man, who was leaning on a staff, and listening very attentively, with his head stretched forward, and one hand at his ear, because, for the last twenty years, he had been getting rather deaf.

"And what do you say, venerable sir?" inquired he. "In your younger days, I should imagine, you must frequently have seen the winged steed!"

"Ah, young stranger, my memory is very poor!" said the aged man. "When I was a lad, if I remember rightly, I used to believe there was such a horse, and so did everybody else. But, nowadays, I hardly know what to think, and very seldom think about the winged horse at all. If I ever saw the creature, it was a long, long while ago; and to tell you the truth, I doubt whether I ever did see him. One day, to be sure, when I was quite a youth, I remember seeing some hoof-tramps round about the brink of the fountain. Pegasus might have made those hoof-marks; and so might some other horse."

"And have you never seen him, my fair maiden?" asked Bellerophon of the girl, who stood with the pitcher on her head, while this talk went on. "You certainly could see Pegasus, if anybody can, for your eyes are very bright."

"Once I thought I saw him," replied the maiden, with a smile and a blush. "It was either Pegasus, or a large white bird, a very great way up in the air. And one other time, as I was coming to the fountain with my pitcher, I heard a neigh. Oh, such a brisk and melodious neigh as that was! My very heart leaped with delight at the sound. But, it startled me, nevertheless, so that I ran home without filling my pitcher."

"That was truly a pity," said Bellerophon.

And he turned to the child, whom I mentioned at the beginning of the story, and who was gazing at him, as children are apt to gaze at strangers, with his rosy mouth wide open.

"Well, my little fellow," cried Bellerophon, playfully pulling one of his curls, "I suppose you have often seen the winged horse."

"That I have," answered the child very readily. "I saw him yesterday, and many times before."

"You are a fine little man!" said Bellerophon, drawing the child closer to him. "Come, tell me all about it."

"Why," replied the child, "I often come here to sail little boats in the fountain, and to gather pretty pebbles out of its basin. And sometimes, when I look down into the water, I see the image of the winged horse, in the picture of the sky that is there. I wish he would come down and take me on his back, and let me ride him up to the moon! But, if I so much as stir to look at him, he flies far away out of sight."

And Bellerophon put his faith in the child, who had seen the image of Pegasus in the water, and in the maiden who had heard him neigh so melodiously, rather than in the middle-aged clown, who believed only in cart horses, or in the old man who had forgotten the beautiful things of his youth.

Therefore, he haunted about the Fountain of Pirene for a great many days afterwards. He kept continually on the watch, looking upward at the sky, or else down into the water, hoping forever that he should see either the reflected image of the winged horse ,or the marvelous reality. He held the bridle, with its bright gems and golden bit, always ready in his hand. The rustic people, who dwelt in the neighborhood, and drove their cattle to the fountain to drink, would often laugh at poor Bellerophon, and sometimes take him pretty severely to task. They told him that an ablebodied young man, like himself, ought to have better business than to be wasting his time in such idle pursuit. They offered to sell him a horse, if he wanted one; and when Bellerophon declined the purchase, they tried to drive a bargain with him for his fine bridle.

Even the country boys thought him so very foolish that they used to have a great deal of sport about him, and were rude enough not to care a fig, although Bellerophon saw and heard it. One little urchin, for example, would play Pegasus, and cut the oddest imaginable capers, by way of flying; while one of his schoolfellows would scamper after him holding forth a twist of bulrushes, which was intended to represent Bellerophon's ornamental bridle. But the gentle child, who had seen the picture of Pegasus in the water, comforted the young stranger more than all the naughty boys could torment him. The dear little fellow, in his play hours, often sat down beside him, and without speaking a word, would look down into the fountain and up towards the sky, with so innocent a faith, that Bellerophon could not help feeling encouraged.

Well was it for Bellerophon that the child had grown so fond of him, and was never weary of keeping him company. Every morning the child gave him a new hope to put in his bosom, instead of yesterday's withered one.

"Dear Bellerophon," he would cry, looking up hopefully into his face, " I think we shall see Pegasus today!"

One morning the child spoke to Bellerophon even more hopefully than usual.

"Dear, dear Bellerophon," cried he, "I know not why it is, but I feel as if we shall certainly see Pegasus today!"

And all that day he would not stir a step from Bellerophon's side; so they ate a crust of bread together, and drank some of the water from the fountain. In the afternoon, there they sat, and

Bellerophon had thrown his arm around the child, who likewise had put one of his little hands into Bellerophon's. The latter was lost in his own thoughts, and was fixing his eyes vacantly on the trunks of the trees that overshadowed the fountain, and on the grapevines that clambered up among the branches. But the gentle child was gazing down into the water. He was grieved, for Bellerophon's sake, that the hope of another day should be deceived, like so many before it; and two or three quiet teardrops fell from his eyes, and mingled with what were said to be the many tears of Pirene, when she wept for her slain children.

But, when he least thought of it, Bellerophon felt the pressure of the child's little hand, and heard a soft, almost breathless whisper.

"See there, dear Bellerophon, there is an image in the water!"

The young man looked down into the dimpling mirror of the fountain, and saw what he took to be the reflection of a bird which seemed to be flying at a great height in the air, with a gleam of sunshine on its snowy or silvery wings.

"What a splendid bird it must be!" said he. "And how very large it looks, though it must really be flying higher than the clouds!"

"It makes me tremble!" whispered the child. "I am afraid to look up into the air! It is very beautiful, and yet I dare only look at its image in the water. Dear Bellerophon, do you not see that it is not bird? It is the winged horse Pegasus!"

Bellerophon's heart began to throb! He gazed keenly upward, but could not see the winged creature, whether bird or horse; because, just then, it had plunged into the fleecy depths of a summer cloud. It was but a moment, however, before the object reappeared, sinking lightly down out of the cloud, although still a vast distance from the earth. Bellerophon caught the child in his arms, and shrank back with him, so that they were both hidden among the thick shrubbery which grew all around the fountain. Not that he was afraid of any harm, but he dreaded lest, if Pegasus caught a glimpse of them, he would fly far away, and alight in some inaccessible mountaintop. For it really was the winged horse. After they had expected him so long, he was coming to quench his thirst with the water of Pirene.

Nearer and nearer came the aerial wonder, flying in great circles, as you may have seen a dove when about to alight. Downward came Pegasus, in those wide, sweeping circles, which grew narrower, and narrower still, as he gradually approached the earth. The nigher the view of him, the more beautiful he was, and the more marvelous the sweep of his silvery wings. At last, with so slight a pressure as hardly to bend the grass about the fountain, or imprint a hoof-tramp in the sand of its margin, he alighted, and, stooping his wild head, began to drink. He drew in the water, with long and pleasant sighs, and tranquil pauses of enjoyment; and then another draught, and another, and another. For, nowhere in the world, or up among the clouds, did Pegasus love any water as he loved this of Pirene. And when his thirst was slaked, he cropped a few of the honey blossoms of the clover, delicately tasting them, but not caring to make a hearty meal, because the herbage, just beneath the clouds, on the lofty sides of Mount Helicon, suited his palate better than this ordinary grass.

After thus drinking to his heart's content, and in his dainty fashion, condescending to take a little food, the winged horse began to caper to and fro, and dance, as it were, out of mere idleness and sport. There was never a more playful creature made than this very Pegasus. So there he frisked, in a way that delights me to think about, fluttering his great wings as lightly as ever did a linnet, and running little races, half on earth and half in air, and which I know not whether to call a flight or a gallop. When a creature is perfectly able to fly, he sometimes chooses to run, just for the pastime of the thing; and so did Pegasus, although it cost him some little trouble to keep his hoofs so near the ground. Bellerophon, meanwhile, holding the child's hand, peeped forth from the shrubbery, and thought that never was any sight so beautiful as this, nor ever a horse's eyes so wild and spirited as those of Pegasus. It seemed a sin to think of bridling him and riding on his back.

Once or twice, Pegasus stopped, and snuffed the air, pricking up his ears, tossing his head, and turning it on all sides, as if he partly suspected some mischief or other. Seeing nothing, however, and hearing no sound, he soon began his antics again.

At length—not that he was weary, but only idle and luxurious—Pegasus folded his wings, and lay down on the soft green turf. But, being too full of aerial life to remain quiet for many moments together, he soon rolled over on his back, with his four slender legs in the air. It was beautiful to see him, this one solitary creature, whose mate had never been created, but who needed no companion, and, living a great many hundred years, was as happy as the centuries were long. The more he did such things as mortal horses are accustomed to do, the less earthly and the more wonderful he seemed. Bellerophon and the child almost held their breath, partly from a delightful awe, but still more because they dreaded lest the slightest stir or murmur should send him up, with the speed of an arrow-flight into the farthest blue of the sky.

Finally, when he had had enough of rolling over and over, Pegasus turned himself about, and, indolently, like an other horse, put out his forelegs, in order to rise from the ground; and Bellerophon, who had guessed that he would do so, darted suddenly from the thicket, and leaped astride of his back.

Yes, there he sat, on the back of the winged horse!

But what a bound did Pegasus make, when, for the first time, he felt the weight of a mortal man upon his loins! A bound, indeed! Before he had time to draw a breath, Bellerophon found himself five hundred feet aloft, and still shooting upward, while the winged horse snorted and trembled with terror and anger. Upward he went, up, up, up, until he plunged into the cold misty bosom of a cloud, at which, only a little while before, Bellerophon had been gazing, and fancying it a very pleasant spot. Then again, out of the heart of the cloud, Pegasus shot down like a thunderbolt, as if he meant to dash both himself and his rider headlong against a rock. Then he went through about a thousand of the wildest caprioles that had ever been performed either by a bird or a horse.

I cannot tell you half that he did. He skimmed straightforward, and sideways, and backward. He reared himself erect, with his forelegs on a wreath of mist and his hind legs on nothing at all. He flung his heels behind, and put his head between his legs, with his wings pointing right upward. At about two miles' height above the earth, he turned a somerset, so that Bellerophon's heels were where his head should have been, and he seemed to look down into the sky, instead of up. He twisted his head about, and looking Bellerophon in the face, with fire flashing from his eyes, made a terrible attempt to bite him. He fluttered his pinions so wildly that one of the silver feathers was shaken out, and, floating earthward, was picked up by the child, who kept it as long as he lived, in memory of Pegasus and Bellerophon.

But the latter (who, as you may judge, was as good a horseman as ever galloped) had been watching his opportunity, and at last clapped the golden bit of the enchanted bridle between the winged steed's jaws. No sooner was this done, than Pegasus became as manageable as if he had taken food all his life out of Bellerophon's hand. To speak what I really feel, it was almost a sadness to see so wild a creature grow suddenly so tame. And Pegasus seemed to feel it so, likewise. He looked round to Bellerophon with tears in his beautiful eyes instead of the fire that so recently flashed from them. But when Bellerophon patted his head, and spoke a few authoritative, yet kind and soothing words; another look came into the eyes of Pegasus; for he was glad at heart, after so many lonely centuries, to have found a companion and a master.

Thus it always is with winged horses, and with all such wild and solitary creatures. If you can catch and overcome them, it is the surest way to win their love.

Strider—The Story of a Horse

[LEO TOLSTOY]

Higher and higher receded the sky, wider and wider spread the streak of dawn, whiter grew the pallid silver of the dew, more lifeless the sickle of the moon, and more vocal the forest. People began to get up, and in the owner's stable-yard the sounds of snorting, the rustling of litter, and even the shrill angry neighing of horses crowded together and at variance about something, grew more and more frequent.

"Hold on! Plenty of time! Hungry?" said the old huntsman, quickly opening the creaking gate. "Where are you going?" he shouted, threateningly raising his arm at a mare that was pushing through the gate.

The keeper, Nester, wore a short Cossack coat with an ornamental leather girdle, had a whip slung over his shoulder, and a hunk of bread wrapped in a cloth stuck in his girdle. He carried a saddle and bridle in his arms.

The horses were not at all frightened or offended at the horseman's sarcastic tone: they pretended that it was all the same to them and moved leisurely away from the gate; only one old brown mare, with a thick mane, laid back an ear and quickly turned her back on him. A small filly standing behind her and not at all concerned in the matter took this opportunity to whinny and kick out at a horse that happened to be near.

"Now then!" shouted the keeper still louder and more sternly, and he went to the opposite corner of the yard.

Of all the horses in the enclosure (there were about a hundred of them), a piebald gelding, standing by himself in a corner under the penthouse and licking an oak post with half-closed eyes, displayed least impatience.

It is impossible to say what flavor the piebald gelding found in the post, but his expression was serious, and thoughtful while he licked.

"Stop that!" shouted the groom, drawing nearer to him and putting the saddle and a glossy saddle-cloth on the manure heap beside him.

The piebald gelding stopped licking and without moving gave Nester a long look. The gelding did not laugh, nor grow angry, nor frown, but his whole belly heaved with a profound sigh and he turned away. The horseman put his arm round the gelding's neck and placed the bridle on him.

"What are you sighing for?" said Nester.

The gelding switched his tail as if to say, "Nothing in particular, Nester!" Nester put the saddle-cloth and saddle on him, and this caused the gelding to lay back his ears, probably to express dissatisfaction, but he was only called a "good-for-nothing" for it and his saddle-girths were tightened.

At this the gelding blew himself out, but a finger was thrust into his mouth and a knee hit him in the stomach, so that he had to let out his breath. In spite of this, when the saddlecloth was being buckled on he again laid back his ears and even looked round. Though he knew it would do no good he considered it necessary to show that it was disagreeable to him and that he would always express his dissatisfaction with it. When he was saddled he thrust forward his swollen-off foot and began champing his bit, this too for some reason of his own, for he ought to have known by that time that a bit cannot have any flavor at all.

Nester mounted the gelding by the short stirrup, unwound his long whip, straightened his coat out from under his knee, seated himself in the manner peculiar to coachmen, huntsman, and horsemen, and jerked the reins. The gelding lifted his head to show his readiness to go where ordered, but did not move. He knew that before starting there would be much shouting and that Nester, from the seat on his back, would give many orders to Vaska, the other groom, and to the horses. And Nester did shout: "Vaska! Hullo, Vaska. Have you let out the brood mares? Where are you going, you devil? Now then! Are you asleep? . . . Open the gate! Let the brood mares get out first!" and so on.

The gate creaked. Vaska, cross and sleepy, stood at the gate post holding his horse by the bridle and letting the other horses pass out. The horses followed one another and stepped carefully over the straw, smelling at it: fillies, yearling colts with their manes and tails cut, suckling foals, and mares in foal carrying their burden heedfully passed one by one through the gateway. The fillies sometimes crowded together in twos and threes, throwing their heads across one another's backs and hitting their hoofs against the gate, for which they received a rebuke from the grooms every time. The foals sometimes darted under the legs of the wrong mares and neighed loudly in response to the short whinny of their own mothers.

A playful filly directly had got out at the gate, bent her head sideways, kicked up her hind legs, and squealed, but all the same she did not dare to run ahead of old dappled Zhuldyba who at a slow and heavy pace, swinging her belly from side to side, marched as usual ahead of all the other horses.

In a few minutes the enclosure that had been so animated became deserted, the posts stood gloomily under the empty penthouse, and only trampled straw mixed with manure was to be seen. Used as he was to that desolate sight it probably depressed the piebald gelding. As if making a bow he slowly lowered his head and raised it again, sighed as deeply as the tightly drawn girth would allow, and hobbling along on his stiff and crooked legs, shambled after the herd, bearing old Nester on his bony back.

"I know that as soon as we get out on the road he will begin to strike a light and smoke his wooden pipe with its brass mountings and little chain," thought the gelding. "I am glad of it because early in the morning when it is dewy I like that smell, it reminds me of much that was pleasant. But it's annoying that when his pipe is between his teeth the old man always begins to swagger and thinks himself somebody and sits sideways, always sideways— and that side hurts. However, it can't be helped! Suffering for the pleasure of others is nothing new to me. I have even begun to find a certain equine pleasure in it. Let him swagger, poor fellow! Of course he can only do that when he is alone and no one see him—let him sit sideways!" thought the gelding, and stepping carefully on his crooked legs he went along the middle of the road.

II

Having driven the horses to the riverside where they were to graze, Nester dismounted and unsaddled. Meanwhile the herd had begun gradually to spread over the untrampled meadow, covered with dew and by the mist that rose from it and the encircling river.

When he had taken the bridle off the piebald gelding, Nester scratched him under the neck, in response to which the gelding expressed his gratitude and satisfaction by closing his eyes. "He likes it, the old dog!" muttered Nester. The gelding, however, did not really care for the scratching at all and pretended that it was agreeable merely out of courtesy. He nodded his head in assent to Nester's words, but suddenly Nester, quite unexpectedly and without any reason, perhaps imagining that too much familiarity might give the gelding a wrong idea of his importance, pushed the gelding's head away from himself without any warning and, swinging the bridle, struck him painfully with the buckle on his lean leg, and then without saying a word went up to the hillock to a tree stump beside which he generally seated himself.

Though this action grieved the piebald gelding he gave no indication of it, but, leisurely switching his scanty tail, sniffed at something and, biting off some wisps of grass merely to divert his mind, walked to the river. He took no notice whatever of the antics of the young mares, colts, and foals around him, who were filled with the joy of the morning; and knowing that, especially at his age, it is healthier to have a good drink on an empty stomach and to eat afterwards, he chose a spot where the bank was widest and least steep, and wetting his hoofs and fetlocks, dipped his muzzle in the water and began to suck it up through his torn lips, to expand his filling sides, and from pleasure to switch his scanty tail with its half bald stump.

An aggressive chestnut filly, who always teased the old fellow and did all kinds of unpleasant things to him, now came up to him in the water as if attending to some business of her own but in reality merely to foul the water before his nose. But the piebald gelding, who had already had his fill, as though not noticing the filly's intention quietly drew one foot after the other out of the mud in which they had sunk, jerked his head, and stepping aside from the youthful crowd, started grazing. Sprawling his feet apart in different ways and not trampling the grass needlessly, he went on eating without unbending himself for exactly three hours.

Having eaten till his belly hung down from his steep skinny ribs like a sack, he balanced himself equally on his four sore legs so as to have a little pain as possible, especially in his off foreleg which was the weakest, and fell asleep.

Old age is sometimes majestic, sometimes ugly, and sometimes pathetic. But old age can be both ugly and majestic, and the gelding's old age was just of that kind.

He was tall, rather over fifteen hands high. His spots were black, or rather they had been black, but had now turned a dirty brown. He had three spots, one on his head, starting from a crooked bald patch on the side of his nose and reaching halfway down his neck. His long mane, filled with burrs, was white in some places and brownish in others. Another spot extended down his off side to the middle of his belly; the third, on his croup, touched part of his tail and went halfway down his quarters. The rest of the tail was whitish and speckled. The big bony head, with deep hollows over the eyes and a black hanging lip that had been torn at some time, hung low and heavily on his neck, which was so lean that it looked as though it were carved of wood. The pendant lip revealed a blackish bitten tongue and the yellow stumps of the worn lower teeth. The ears, one of which was slip, hung low on either side, and only occasionally moved lazily to drive away the pestering flies. Of the forelock, one tuft which was still long hung back behind an ear; the uncovered forehead was dented and rough, and the skin hung down like bags on his broad jawbones. The veins of his neck had grown knotty and twitched and shuddered at every touch of a fly. The expression of his face was one of stern patience, thoughtfulness, and suffering.

His forelegs were crooked to a bow at the knees, there were swellings over both hoofs, and on one leg, on which the piebald spot reached halfway down, there was a swelling at the knee as big as a fist. The hind legs were in better condition, but apparently long ago his haunches had been so rubbed that in places the hair would not grow again. The leanness of his body made all four legs look disproportionately long. The ribs, though straight, were so exposed and the skin so tightly drawn over them, that it seemed to have dried fast to the spaces between. His back and withers were covered with marks of old lashings, and there was a fresh sore behind, still swollen and festering; the black dock of his tail, which showed the vertebrae, hung down long and almost bare. On his dark-brown croup— near the tail—was a scar, as though of a bite, the size of a man's hand and covered with white hair. Another scarred sore was visible on one of his shoulders. His tail and hocks were dirty because of chronic bowel troubles. The hair on the whole body, though short, stood out straight. Yet in spite of the hideous old age of this horse one involuntarily paused the reflect when one saw him, and an expert would have said at once that he had been a remarkably fine horse in his day. The expert would even have said that there was only one breed in Russia that could furnish such breadth of bone, such immense knees, such hoofs, such slender cannons, such a well-shaped neck, and above all such a skull, such eyes—large, black, and clear—and such a thoroughbred network of veins on head and neck, and such delicate skin and hair.

There was really something majestic in that horse's figure and in the terrible union in him of repulsive indications of decrepitude, emphasized by the motley color of his hair, and his manner which expressed the self-confidence and calm assurance that go with beauty and strength. Like a living ruin he stood alone in the midst of the dewy meadow, while not far from him could be heard the tramping, snorting, and youthful neighing and whinnying of the scattered herd.

III

The sun had risen above the forest and now shone brightly on the grass and the winding river.

The dew was drying up and condensing into drops, the last of the morning mist was dispersing like tiny smoke clouds. The cloudlets were becoming curly but there was as yet no wind. Beyond the river the verdant rye stood bristling, its ears curling into little horns, and there was an odor of fresh verdure and blossom. A cuckoo called rather hoarsely from the forest, and Nester, lying on his back in the grass, was counting the calls to ascertain how many years he still had to live. The larks were rising over the rye and the meadow. A belated hare, finding himself among the horses, leaped into the open, sat down by a bush, and pricked his ears to listen. Vaska fell asleep with his head in the grass; the fillies, making a still wider circle around him, scattered over the field below. The old mares when about snorting and made a shiny track across the dewy grass, always choosing a place where no one would disturb them. They no longer grazed but only nibbled at choice tufts of grass. The whole herd was moving imperceptibly in one direction.

And again it was old Zhuldyba who, stepping sedately in front of the others, showed the possibility of going farther. Black Mushka, a young mare who had foaled for the first time, with uplifted tail kept whinnying and snorting at her bluish foal; the young filly Satin, sleek and brilliant, bending her head till her black silky forelock hid her forehead and eyes, played with the grass, nipping off a little and tossing it and stamping her leg with its shaggy fetlock all wet with dew. One of the older foals, probably imagining he was playing some kind of game, with his curly tail raised like a plume, ran for the twenty-sixth time round his mother, who quietly went on grazing, having grown accustomed to her son's ways, and only occasionally glanced askance at him with one of her large black eyes.

One of the very youngest foals, black, with a big head, a tuft sticking up in astonishment between his ears, and a little tail still twisted to one side as it had been in his mother's womb, stood motionless, his ears pricked and his dull eyes fixed, gazing at the frisking and prancing foal—whether admiring or condemning him it is hard to say. Some of the foals were sucking and butting with their noses, some— heaven knows why—despite their mother's call were running at an awkward little trot in quite the opposite direction as if searching for something and then, for no apparent reason, stopping and neighing with desperate shrillness. Some lay on their sides in a row, some were learning to eat grass, some again were scratching themselves behind their ears with their hind legs. Two mares still in foal were walking apart from the rest and while slowly moving their legs continued to graze. The others evidently respected their condition, and none of the young ones ventured to come near to disturb them. If any saucy youngsters thought of approaching them, the mere movement of an ear or tail sufficed to show them all how improper such behavior was.

The colts and yearling fillies, pretending to be grownup and sedate, rarely jumped or joined the merry company. They grazed in a dignified manner, curving their close-cropped swan-like necks, and flourished their little broom-like tails as if they also had long ones. Just like the grownups they lay down, rolled over, or rubbed one another. The merriest group was composed of the two- and three-year-old fillies and mares not yet in foal. They almost always walked about together like a separate merry virgin crowd. Among them you could hear sounds of tramping, whinnying, neighing, and snorting. They drew close together, put their heads over one another's necks, sniffed at one another, jumped, and sometimes at a semi-trot, semi-amble, with tails lifted like an oriflamme, raced proudly and coquettishly past their companions. The most beautiful and spirited of them was the mischievous chestnut filly. What she devised the others did; wherever she went the whole crowd of beauties followed. That morning the naughty one was in a specially playful mood. She was seized with a joyous fit, just as human beings sometimes are. Already at the riverside she had played a trick on the old gelding, and after that she ran along through the water pretending to be frightened by something, gave a hoarse squeal, and raced full speed into the field so that Vaska had to gallop after her and the others who followed her. Then after grazing a little she began rolling, then teasing the old mares by dashing in front of them, then she drove away a small foal from the dam and chased it as if meaning to bite it. Its mother was frightened and stopped grazing, while the little foal cried in a piteous tone, but the mischievous one did not touch him at all, she only wanted to frighten him and give a performance for the benefit of her companions, who watched her escapade approvingly. Then she set out to turn the head of a little roan horse with which a peasant was ploughing in a rye field far beyond the river. She stopped, proudly lifted her head somewhat to one side, shook herself, and neighed in a sweet, tender, long-drawn voice. Mischief, feeling, and a certain sadness were expressed in that call. There was in it the desire for and the promise of love, and a pining for it.

"There in the thick reeds is a corn-crake running backwards and forwards and calling passionately to his mate; there is the cuckoo, and the quails are singing of love, and the flowers are sending their fragrant dust to each other by the wind. And I too am young and beautiful and strong." The mischievous one's voice said, "but it has not yet been allowed me to know the sweetness of that feeling, and not only to experience it, but no lover—not a single one— has ever seen me!"

And this neighing, sad and youthful and fraught with feeling, was borne over the lowland and the field to the roan horse far away. He pricked up his ears and stopped. The peasant kicked him with his bast shoe, but the little horse was so enchanted by the silvery sound of the distant neighing that he neighed too. The peasant grew angry, pulled at the reins, and kicked the little roan so painfully in the stomach with his bast shoes that he could not finish his neigh and walked on. But the little roan felt a sense of sweetness and sadness, and for a long time the sounds of unfinished and passionate neighing, and of the peasant's angry voice, were carried from the distant rye field over to the herd.

If the sound of her voice alone so overpowered the little roan that he forgot his duty, what would have happened had he seen the naughty beauty as she stood pricking her ears, breathing in the air with dilated nostrils, ready to run, trembling with her whole beautiful body, and calling to him?

But the mischievous one did not brood long over her impressions. When the neighing of the roan died away she gave another scornful neigh, lowered her head, and began pawing the ground, and then she went to wake and tease the piebald gelding. The piebald gelding was the constant martyr and butt of those happy youngsters. He suffered more from them than at the hands of men. He did no harm to either. People needed him, but why should these young horses torment him?

IV

He was old, they were young; he was lean, they were sleek; he was miserable, they were gay; and so he was quite alien to them, an outsider, an utterly different creature whom it was impossible for them to pity. Horses only have pity on themselves and very occasionally on those in whose skins they can easily imagine themselves to be. But was it the old gelding's fault that he was old, poor, and ugly?

One might think not, but in equine ethics it was, and only those were right who were strong, young, and happy—those who had life still before them, whose every muscle quivered with superfluous energy, and whose tails stood erect. Maybe the piebald gelding himself understood this and in his quiet moments was ready to agree that it was his fault that he had already lived his life, and that he had to pay for that life, but after all he was a horse and often could not suppress a sense of resentment, sadness, and indignation when he looked at those youngsters who tormented him for what would befall them all at the end of their lives. Another cause of the horse's lack of pity was their aristocratic pride. Every one of them traced back its pedigree, through father or mother, to the famous Creamy, while the piebald was of un-known parentage. He was a chance comer, purchased three years before at a fair for eighty assignat rubles.

The chestnut filly, as if taking a stroll, passed close by the piebald gelding's nose and pushed him. He knew at once was it was, and without opening his eyes laid back his ears and showed his teeth. The filly wheeled round as if to kick him. The gelding opened his eyes and stepped aside. He did not want to sleep anymore and began to graze. The mischief-maker, fol-lowed by her companions, again approached the geld-ing. A very stupid two-year-old white-spotted filly who always imitated the chestnut in everything went up with her and, as imitators always do, went to greater lengths than the instigator. The chestnut always went up as if intent on business of her own and passed by the gelding's nose without looking at him, so that he really did not know whether to be angry or not, and that was really funny.

She did the same now, but the white-spotted one, who followed her and had grown particularly lively, bumped right against the gelding with her chest. He again showed his teeth, whinnied, and with an agility one could not have expected of him, rushed after her and bit her flank. The white-spotted one kicked out with all her strength and dealt the old horse a heavy blow on his thin bare ribs. He snorted heavily and was going to rush at her again but bethought himself, and drawing a deep sigh, stepped aside. The whole crowd of young ones must have taken as a personal affront the impertinence the piebald gelding had permitted himself to offer to the white-spotted one and for the rest of the day did not let him graze in peace for a moment, so that the keeper had to quiet them several times and could not understand what had come over them.

The gelding felt so offended that he went up himself to Nester when the old man was getting ready to drive the horses home and felt happier and quieter when he was saddled and the old man had mounted him.

God knows what the gelding was thinking as he carried old Nester on his back; whether he thought bitterly of the pertinacious and merciless youngsters or forgave his tormentors with the contemptuous and silent pride suited old age. At all events he did not betray his thoughts till he reached home.

That evening as Nester drove the horses past the huts of the domestic serfs, he noticed a peasant horse and cart tethered to his porch; some friends had come to see him. When driving the horses in he was in such a hurry that he let the gelding in without unsaddling him and, shouting to Vaska to do it, shut the gate and went to his friends. Whether because of the affront to the white-spotted filly—Creamy's great-granddaughter—by that "mangy trash" bought at the horse fair, who did not know his father or mother, and the consequent outrage to the aristocratic sentiment of the whole herd, or because the gelding with his high saddle and without a rider presented a strangely fantastic spectacle to the horses, at any rate something quite unusual occurred that night in the paddock. All the horses, young and old, ran after the gelding, showing their teeth and driving him all round the yard; one heard the sound of hoofs striking against his bare ribs, and his deep moaning. He could no longer endure this, nor could he avoid the blows. He stopped in the middle of the paddock, his face expressing first the repulsive weak malevolence of helpless old age, and then despair: he dropped his ears, and then something happened that caused all the horses to quiet down. The oldest of the mares, Vyazapurikha, went up to the gelding, sniffed at him, and sighed. The gelding sighed too.

V

In the middle of the moonlit paddock stood the tall gaunt figure of the gelding, still wearing the high saddle with its prominent peak at the bow. The horses stood motionless and in deep silence around him as if they were learning something new and unexpected.

This is what they learned from him. . . .

First night

Yes, I am the son of Affable I and of Baba. My pedigree name is Muzhik, and I was nicknamed Strider by the crowd because of my long and sweeping strides, the like of which was nowhere to be found in all Russia. There is no more thoroughbred horse in the world. I should never have told you this. What good would it have done? You would never have recognized me: even Vyazapurikha, who was with me in Khrenovoa, did not recognize me till now. You would not have believed me if Vyazapurikha were not here to be my witness, and I should never have told you this. I don't need equine sympathy. But you wished it. Yes, I am that Strider whom connoisseurs are looking for and cannot find—that Strider whom the count himself knew and got rid of from his stud because I outran Swan, his favorite.

When I was born, I did not know what "piebald" meant—I thought I was just a horse. I remember that the first remark we heard about my color struck my mother and me deeply.

I suppose I was born in the night; by the morning, having been licked over by my mother, I already stood on my feet. I remember I kept wanting something and that everything seemed very surprising and yet very simple. Our stalls opened into a long war passage and had latticed doors through which everything could be seen.

My mother offered me her teats but I was still so innocent that I poked my nose now between her forelegs and now under her udder. Suddenly she glanced at the latticed door and, lifting her leg over me, stepped aside. The groom on duty was looking into our stall through the lattice.

"Why, Baba has foaled!" he said, and began to draw the bolt. He came in over the fresh bedding and put his arms around me. "Just look, Taras!" he shouted, "what a piebald he is—a regular magpie!"

I darted away from him and fell on my knees.

"Look at him—the little devil!"

My mother became disquieted but did not take my part; she only stepped a little to one side with a very deep sigh. Other grooms came to look at me, and one of them ran to tell the stud groom.

Everybody laughed when they looked at my spots, and they gave me all kinds of strange names, but neither I not my mother understood these words. Till then there had been no piebalds among all my relatives. We did not think there was anything bad in it. Everybody even praised my strength and my form.

"See what a frisky fellow!" said the groom. "There's no holding him."

Before long the stud groom came and began to express astonishment at my color; he even seemed aggrieved.

"And who does the little monster take after?" he said. "The general won't keep him in the stud. Oh, Baba, you have played me a trick!" he addressed my mother. "You might at least have dropped one with just a star—but this one is all piebald!"

My mother did not reply but as usual on such occasions drew a sigh. "And what devil does he take after—he's just like a peasant horse!" he continued. "He can't be left in the stud—he'd shame us. But he's well built—very well!" said he, and so did everyone who saw me.

A few days later the general himself came and looked at me, and again everyone seemed horrified at something, and abused me and my mother for the color of my hair. "But he's a fine colt—very fine!" said all who saw me.

Until spring we all lived separately in the brood mares' stable, each with our mother, and only occasionally when the snow on the stable roofs began to melt in the sun were we let out with our mothers into the large paddock strewn with fresh straw. There

I first came to know all my near and my distant relations. Here I saw all the famous mares of the day
coming out from different doors with their little
foals. There was the old mare Dutch, Fly (Creamy's
daughter), Ruddy the riding horse, Wellwisher—all
celebrities at that time. They all gathered together
with their foals, walking about in the sunshine,
rolling on the fresh straw and sniffing at one another
like ordinary horses. I have never forgotten the sight
of that paddock full of the beauties of that day. It
seems strange to you to think and hard to believe,
that I was ever young and frisky, but it was so. This
same Vyazapurikha was then a yearling filly whose
mane had just been cut; a dear, merry, lively little
thing, but—and I do not say it to offend her—although among you she is now considered a remarkable thoroughbred she was then among the poorest
horses in the stud. She will herself confirm this.

My mottled appearance, which men so disliked,
was very attractive to all the horses; they all came
round me, admired me, and frisked about with me.
I began to forget what men said about my mottled
appearance and felt happy. But I soon experienced
the first sorrow of my life and the cause of it was my
mother. When the thaw had set in, the sparrows
twittered under the eaves, spring was felt more
strongly in the air, and my mother's treatment of me
changed.

Her whole disposition changed: she would frisk about without any reason and run round the yard, which did not at all accord with her dignified age; then she would consider and begin to neigh, and would bite and kick her sister mares, and then begin to sniff at me and snort discontentedly; then on going out into the sun she would lay her head across the shoulder of her cousin, Lady Merchant, dreamily rub her back, and push me away from her teats.

One day the stud groom came and had a halter put on her and she was led out of the stall. She neighed and I answered and rushed after her, but she did not even look back at me. The strapper, Taras, seized me in his arms while they were closing the door after my mother had been led out.

I bolted and upset the strapper on the straw, but the door was shut and I could only hear the receding sound of my mother's neighing; and that neigh did not sound like a call to me but had another expression. Her voice was answered from afar by a powerful voice—that of Dobry I, as I learned later, who was being led by two grooms—one on each side, to meet my mother.

I don't remember how Taras got out of my stall: I felt too sad, for I knew that I had lost my mother's love forever. "And it's all because I am piebald!" I thought, remembering what people said about my color, and such passionate anger overcame me that I began to beat my head and knees against the walls of the stall and continued till I was sweating all over and quite exhausted.

After a while my mother came back to me. I heard her run up the passage at a trot and with an unusual gait. They opened the door for her and I hardly knew her—she had grown so much younger and more beautiful. She sniffed at me, snorted, and began to whinny. Her whole demeanor showed that she no longer loved me.

She told me of Dobry's beauty and her love of him. Those meetings continued and the relations between my mother and me grew colder and colder.

Soon after that we were let out to pasture. I now discovered new joys which made up to me for the loss of my mother's love. I had friends and companions. Together we learned to eat grass, to neigh like the grownups, and to gallop round our mothers with lifted tails. That was a happy time. Everything was forgiven me, everybody loved me, admired me, and looked indulgently at anything I did. But that did not last long.

Soon afterwards something dreadful happened to me.

. . . The gelding heaved a deep sigh and walked away from the other horses.

The dawn had broken long before. The gates creaked. Nester came in, and the horses separated. The keeper straightened the saddle on the gelding's back and drove the horses out.

VI

Second night

As soon as the horses had been driven in they again gathered round the piebald, who continued:

In August they separated me from my mother and I did not feel particularly grieved. I saw that she was again heavy (with my brother, the famous Usan) and that I could no longer be to her what I had been. I was not jealous but felt that I had become indifferent to her. Besides, I knew that having left my mother I should be put in the general division of foals, where we were kept two or three together and were every day let out in a crowd into the open. I was in the same stall with Darling. Darling was a saddle horse, who was subsequently ridden by the emperor and portrayed in pictures and sculpture. At that time he was a mere foal, with a soft glossy coat, a swanlike neck, and straight slender legs taut as the strings of an instrument. He was always lively, good-tempered, and amiable, always ready to gambol, exchange licks, and lay tricks on horse or man. Living together as we did we involuntarily made friends, and our friendship lasted the whole of our youth. He was merry and giddy. Even then he began to make love, courted the fillies, and laughed at my guilelessness. To my misfortune, vanity led me to imitate him, and I was soon carried away and fell in love. And this early tendency of mine was the cause of the greatest change in my fate. It happened that I was carried away. . . . Vyazapurikha was a year older than I, and we were special friends, but towards the autumn I noticed that she began to be shy with me. . . .

But I will not speak of that unfortunate period of my first love; she herself remembers my mad passion, which ended for me in the most important change of my life.

The strappers rushed to drive her away and to beat me. That evening I was shut up in a special stall where I neighed all night as if foreseeing what was to happen next.

In the morning the general, the stud groom, the stablemen and the strappers came into the passage where my stall was, and there was a terrible hubbub. The general said that he would have everybody flogged, and that it would not do to keep young stallions. The stud groom promised that he would have everything attended to. They grew quiet and went away. I did not understand anything, but could see that they were planning something concerning me.

The day after that I ceased neighing forever. I became what I am now.

The whole world changed in my eyes. Nothing mattered anymore; I became self-absorbed and began to brood. At first everything seemed repulsive to me. I even ceased to eat, drink, or walk, and there was no idea of playing. Now and then it occurred to me to give a kick, to gallop, or to start neighing, but immediately came the question: Why? What for? And all my energy died away.

One evening I was being exercised just when the horses were driven back from pasture. I saw in the distance a cloud of dust enveloping the indistinct but familiar outlines of all our brood mares. I heard their cheerful snorting and the trampling of their feet. I stopped, though the cord of the halter by which the groom was leading me cut the nape of my neck, and I gazed at the approaching drove as one gazes at happiness that is lost forever and cannot return. They approached, and I could distinguish one after another all the familiar, beautiful, stately, healthy, sleek figures. Some of them also turned to look at me. I was unconscious of the pain the groom's jerking at my halter inflicted. I forgot myself and from old habit involuntarily neighed and began to trot, but my neighing sounded sad, ridiculous, and meaningless. No one in the drove made sport of me, but I noticed that out of decorum many of them turned away from me. They evidently felt it repugnant, pitiable, indelicate, and above all ridiculous, to look at my thin, expressionless neck, my large head (I had grown lean in the meantime), my long, awkward legs, and the silly awkward gait with which by force of habit I trotted round the groom. No one answered my neighing—they all looked away. Suddenly I understood it all, understood how far I was forever removed from them, and I do not remember how I got home with the groom.

Already before that I had shown a tendency towards gravity and thoughtfulness, but now a decided change came over me. My being piebald, which aroused such curious contempt in men, my terrible and unexpected misfortune, and also my peculiar position in the stud farm which I felt but was unable to explain made me retire into myself. I pondered over the injustice of men, who blamed me for being piebald; I pondered on the inconstancy of mother-love and feminine love in general and on its dependence on physical conditions; and above all I pondered on the characteristics of that strange race of animals with whom we are so closely connected, and whom we call men—those characteristics which were the source of my own peculiar position in the stud farm, which I felt but could not understand.

The meaning of this peculiarity in people and the characteristic on which it is based was shown to me by the following occurrence:

It was in winter at holiday time. I had not been fed or watered all day. As I learned later this happened because the lad who fed us was drunk. That day the stud groom came in, saw that I had no food, began to use bad language about the missing lad, and then went away.

Next day the lad came into our stable with another groom to give us hay. I noticed that he was particularly pale and sad and that in the expression of his long back especially there was something significant which evoked compassion.

He threw the hay angrily over the grating. I made a move to put my head over his shoulder but he struck me such a painful blow on the nose with his fist that I started back. Then he kicked me in the belly with his boot.

"If it hadn't been for this scurvy beast," he said, "nothing would have happened!"

"How's that?" inquired the other groom.

"You see, he doesn't go to look after the count's horses but visits his own twice a day."

"What, have they given him the piebald?" asked the other.

"Given it, or sold it—the devil only knows! The count's horses might all starve—he wouldn't care—

but just dare to leave 'his' colt without food! 'Lie down!' he says, and they begin walloping me! No Christianity in it. He has more pity on a beast than on a man. He must be an infidel—he counted the strokes himself, the barbarian! The general never flogged like that! My whole back is covered with wales. There's no Christian soul in him!"

What they said about flogging and Christianity I understood well enough, but I was quite in the dark as to what they meant by the words "his colt," from which I perceived that people considered that there was some connection between me and the head groom. What the connection was I could not at all understand then. Only much later when they separated me from the other horses did I learn what it meant. At that time I could not at all understand what they meant by speaking of "me" as being a man's property. The words "my" horse applied to me, a live horse, seemed to me as strange as to say "my land," "my air," or "my water."

But those words had an enormous effect on me. I thought of them constantly and only after long and varied relations with men did I at last understand the meaning they attach to these strange words, which indicate that men are guided in life not by deeds but by words. They like not so much to do or abstain from doing anything, as to be able to apply conventional words to different objects. Such words, considered very important among them, are "my" and "mine," which they apply to various things, creatures, or objects; even to land, people, and horses. They have agreed that of any given thing only one person may use the word "mine" and he who in this game of theirs may use that conventional word about the greatest number of things is considered the happiest. Why this is so I do not know, but it is so. For a long time I tried to explain it by some direct advantage they derive from it, but this proved wrong.

For instance, many of those who called me "their" horse did not ride me, quite other people rode me; nor did they feed me—quite other people did that. Again it was not those who called me "their" horse who treated me kindly, but coachmen, veterinaries, and in general, quite other people. Later on, having widened my field of observation, I became convinced that not only as applied to us horses, but in regard to other things, the idea of "mine" has no other basis than a low, mercenary instinct in men, which they call the feeling or right of property. A man who never lives in it says "my house" but only concerns himself with its building and maintenance; and a tradesman talks of "my cloth business" but has none of his clothes made of the best cloth that is in his shop.

There are people who call land theirs, though they have never seen that land and never walked on it. There are people who call other people theirs but have never seen those others, and the whole relationship of the owners to the owned is that they do them harm.

There are men who call women their women or their wives; yet these women live with other men. And men strive in life not to do what they think right but to call as many things as possible "their own."

I am now convinced that in this lies the essential difference between men and us. Therefore, not to speak of other things in which we are superior to men, on this ground alone we may boldly say that in the scale of living creatures we stand higher than man. The activity of men, at any rate of those I have had to do with, is guided by words, while ours is guided by deeds.

It was this right to speak of me as "my horse" that the stud groom had obtained, and that was why he had the stable lad flogged. This discovery much astonished me and, together with the thoughts and opinions aroused in men by my piebald color, and the thoughtfulness produced in me by my mother's betrayal, caused me to become the serious and thoughtful gelding that I am.

I was thrice unfortunate: I was piebald, I was a gelding, and people considered that I did not belong to God and to myself, as is natural to all living creatures, but that I belonged to the stud groom.

Their thinking this about me had many consequences. The first was that I was kept apart from the other horses, was better fed, more often taken out on the line, and was broken in at an earlier age. I was first harnessed in my third year. I remember how the stud groom, who imagined I was his, himself began to harness me with a crowd of other grooms, expecting me to prove unruly or to resist. They put ropes round me to lead me into the shafts, put a cross of broad straps on my back and fastened it to the shafts so that I could not kick, while I was only awaiting an opportunity to show my readiness and love of work.

They were surprised that I started like an old horse. They began to break me and I began to practice trotting. Every day I made greater and greater progress, so that after three months the general himself and many others approved of my pace. But strange to say, just because they considered me not as their own, but as belonging to the head groom, they regarded my paces quite differently.

The stallions who were my brothers were raced, their records were kept, people went to look at them, drove them in gilt sulkies, and expensive horse cloths were thrown over them. I was driven in a common sulky to Chesmenka and other farms on the head groom's business. All this was the result of my being piebald, and especially of my being in their opinion, not the count's, but the head groom's property.

Tomorrow, if we are alive, I will tell you the chief consequence for me of this right of property the head groom considered himself to have. . . .

All that day the horses treated Strider respectfully, but Nester's treatment of him was as rough as ever. The peasant's little roan horse neighed again on coming up to the herd, and the chestnut filly again coquettishly replied to him.

VII

Third night

The new moon had risen and its narrow crescent lit up Strider's figure as he once again stood in the middle of the stable-yard. The other horses crowded round him.

The gelding continued:

For me the most surprising consequence of my not being the count's, nor God's, but the head groom's, was that the very thing that constitutes our chief merit—a fast pace—was the cause of my banishment. They were driving Swan round the track, and the head groom, returning from Chesmenka, drove me up and stopped there. Swan went past. He went well, but all the same he was showing off and had not the exactitude I had developed in myself— so that directly one foot touched the ground another instantaneously lifted and not the lightest effort was lost but every atom of exertion carried me forward. Swan went by us. I pulled towards the ring and the head groom did not check me. "Here, shall I try my piebald?" he shouted, and when next Swan came abreast of us he let me go. Swan was already going fast, and so I was left behind during the first round, but in the second I began to gain on him, drew near to his sulky, drew level—and passed him. They tried us again—it was the same thing. I was the faster. And this dismayed everybody. The general asked that I should be sold at once to some distant place, so that nothing more should be heard of me: "Or else the count will get to know of it and there will be trouble!" So they sold me to a horse dealer as a shaft horse. I did not remain with him long. A hussar who came to buy remounts bought me. All this was so unfair, so cruel, that I was glad when they took me away from Khrenova and parted me forever from all that had been familiar and dear to me. It was too painful for me among them. They had love, honor, freedom, before them! I had labor, humiliation, humiliation, labor, to the end of my life. And why? Because I was piebald, and because of that had to become somebody's horse . . . .

Strider could not continue that evening. An event occurred in the enclosure that upset all the horses. Kupchikha, a mare big with foal, who had stood listening to the story, suddenly turned away and walked slowly into the shed, and there began to groan so that it drew the attention of all the horses. Then she lay down, then got up again, and again lay down. The old mares understood what was happening to her, but the young ones became excited and, leaving the gelding, surrounded the invalid. Towards morning there was a new foal standing unsteadily on its little legs. Nester shouted to the groom, and the mare and foal were taken into a stall and the other horses driven to the pasture without them.

VIII

Fourth night

In the evening when the gate was closed and all had quieted down, the piebald continued:

I have had the opportunity to make many observations both of men and horses during the time I passed from hand to hand.

I stayed longest of all with two masters: a prince (an officer of hussars), and later with an old lady who lived near the church of St. Nicholas the Wonder Worker.

The happiest years of my life I spent with the officer of hussars. Though he was the cause of my ruin, and though he never loved anything or anyone, I loved and still love him for that very reason.

What I liked about him was that he was handsome, happy, rich, and therefore never loved anybody.

You understand that lofty equine feeling of ours. His coldness and my dependence on him gave special strength to my love for him. "Kill me, drive me till my wind is broken!" I used to think in our good days, "and I shall be all the happier."

He bought me from an agent to whom the head groom had sold me for eight hundred rubles, and he did so just because no one else had piebald horses. That was my best time. He had a mistress. I knew this because I took him to her every day and sometimes took them both out.

His mistress was a handsome woman, and he was handsome, and his coachman was handsome, and I loved them all because they were. Life was worth living then. This was how our time was spent: In the morning the groom came to rub me down—not the coachman himself but the groom. The groom was a lad from among the peasants. He would open the door, let out the steam from the horses, throw out the droppings, take off our rugs, and begin to fidget over our bodies with a brush, and lay whitish streaks of dandruff from a currycomb on the boards of the floor that was dented by our rough horseshoes. I would playfully nip his sleeve and paw the ground. Then we were led out one after another to the trough filled with cold water, and the lad would admire the smoothness of my spotted coat which he had polished, my foot with its broad hoof, my legs straight as an arrow, my glossy quarters, and my back wide enough to sleep on. Hay was piled into the high racks, and the oak cribs were filled with oats. Then Feofan, the head coachman, would come in.

Master and coachman resembled each other. Neither of them was afraid of anything or cared for anyone but himself, and for that reason everybody liked them. Feofan wore a red shirt, black velveteen knickerbockers, and a sleeveless coat. I liked it on a holiday when he would come into the stable, his hair pomaded, and wearing his sleeveless coat, and would shout, "Now then, beastie, have you forgotten?" and push me with the handle of the stable fork, never so as to hurt me but just as a joke. I immediately knew that it was a joke and laid back an ear, making my teeth click.

We had a black stallion, who drove in a pair. At night they used to put me in harness with him. That

Polkan, as he was called, did not understand a joke but was simply vicious as the devil. I was in the stall next to his and sometimes we bit each other seriously. Feofan was not afraid of him. He would come up and give a shout: it looked as if Polkan would kill him, but no, he'd miss, and Feofan would put the harness on him.

Once, he and I bolted down Smiths Bridge Street. Neither my master nor the coachman was frightened: they laughed, shouted at the people, checked us, and turned so that no one was run over.

In their service I lost my best qualities and half my life. They ruined me by watering me wrongly, and they foundered me. . . . Still, for all that, it was the best time of my life. At twelve o'clock they would come to harness me, black my hoofs, moisten my forelock and mane, and put me in the shafts.

The sledge was of plaited cane upholstered with velvet. The reins were of silk, the harness had silver buckles, sometimes there was a cover of silken fly-net, and altogether it was such that when all the traces and straps were fastened it was difficult to say where the harness ended and the horse began. We were harnessed at ease in the stable. Feofan would come, broader at the hips than at the shoulders, his red belt up under his arms. He would examine the harness, take his seat, wrap his coat round him, put his foot into the sledge stirrup, let off some joke, and for appearance' sake always hang a whip over his arm though he hardly ever hit me, and would say "Let go!" and, playfully stepping from foot to foot I would move out of the gate, and the cook who had come out to empty the slops would stop on the threshold, and the peasant who had brought wood into the yard would open his eyes wide. We would come out, go a little way, and stop. Footmen would come out and other coachmen, and a chatter would begin. Everybody would wait: Sometimes we had to stand for three hours at the entrance, moving a little way, turning back, and standing again.

At last there would be a stir in the hall: Old Tikhon with his paunch would rush out in his dress coat and cry, "Drive up!" (In those days there was not that stupid way of saying, "Forward!" as if one did not know that we moved forward and not back.) Feofan would cluck, drive up, and the prince would hurry out carelessly, as though there were nothing remarkable about the sledge, or the horse, or Feofan—who bent his back and stretched out his arms so that it seemed it would be impossible for him to keep them long in that position. The prince would have a shako on his head and wear a fur coat with a grey beaver collar hiding his rosy, black–browed, handsome face, that should never have been concealed. He would come out clattering his saber, his spurs, and the brass backs of the heels of his overshoes, stepping over the carpet as if in a hurry and taking no notice of me or Feofan whom everybody but he looked at and admired. Feofan would cluck, I would tug at the reins, and respectably, at a foot pace, we would draw up to the entrance and stop. I would turn my eyes on the prince and jerk my thoroughbred head with its delicate forelock. The prince would be in good spirits and sometimes jest with Feofan. Feofan would reply, half turning his handsome head, and without lowering his arms would make a scarcely perceptible movement with the reins which I understand. And then one, two, three. . . . with ever wider and wider strides, every muscle quivering, and sending the muddy snow against the front of the sledge, I would go. In those days, too, there was none of the present-day stupid habit of crying "Oh!" as if the coachman were in pain, instead of the sensible "Be off! Take care!" Feofan would shout, "Be off!" Look out there!" and the people would step aside and stand craning their necks to see the handsome gelding, the handsome coachman, and the handsome gentleman. . . .

I was particularly fond of passing a trotter. When Feofan and I saw at a distance a turn-out worthy of the effort , we would fly like a whirlwind and gradually gain on it. Now, throwing the dirt right to the back of the sledge, I would draw level with the occupant of the vehicle and snort above his head: Then I would reach the horse's harness and the arch of his troika, and then would no longer see it but only hear its sounds in the distance behind. And the prince, Feofan, and I, would all be silent, and pretend to be merely going on our own business and not even notice those with slow horses whom we happened to meet on our way. I liked to pass another horse but also liked to meet a good trotter. An instant, a sound, a glance, and we had passed each other and were flying in opposite directions . . . .

The gate creaked and voices of Nester and Vaska were heard.

Fifth night

The weather began to break up. It had been dull since morning and there was no dew, but it was warm and the mosquitoes were troublesome. As soon as the horses were driven in they collected round the piebald, and he finished his story as follows:

The happy period of my life was soon over. I lived in that way only two years. Towards the end of the second winter the happiest event of my life occurred, and following it came my greatest misfortune. It was during carnival week. I took the prince to the races. Glossy and Bull were running. I don't know what people were doing in the pavilion, but I know the prince came out and ordered Feofan to drive onto the track. I remember how they took me in and placed me beside Glossy. He was harnessed to a racing sulky and I, just as I was, to a town sledge. I outstripped him at the turn. Roars of laughter and howls of delight greeted me.

When I was led in, a crowd followed me and five or six people offered the prince thousands for me. He only laughed, showing his white teeth. "No," he said, "this isn't a horse, but a friend. I wouldn't sell him for mountains of gold. Au revoir, gentleman!" He unfastened the sledge apron and got in.

"To Ostozenka Street!" That was where his mistress lived, and off we flew. . . .

That was our last happy day. We reached her home. He spoke of her as "his," but she loved someone else and had run away with him. The prince learned this at her lodgings. It was five o'clock, and without unharnessing me he started in pursuit of her. They did what had never been done to me before—struck me with the whip and made me gallop. For the first time I fell out of step and felt ashamed and wished to correct it, but suddenly I heard the prince shout in an unnatural voice: "Get on!" The whip whistled through the air and cut me, and I galloped, striking my foot against the iron front of the sledge. We overtook her after going sixteen miles. I got him there but trembled all night long and could not eat anything. In the morning they gave me water. I drank it and after that was never again the horse that I had been. I was ill, and they tormented me and maimed me—doctoring me, as people call it. My hoofs came off, I had swellings and my legs grew bent; my chest sank in and I became altogether limp and weak. I was sold to a horse dealer who fed me carrots and something else and made something of me quite unlike myself, though good enough to deceive one who did not know. My strength and my pace were gone.

When purchasers came the dealer also tormented me by coming into my stall and beating me with a heavy whip to frighten me and madden me. Then he would rub down the stripes on my coat and lead me out.

An old woman bought me of him. She always drove to the Church of St. Nicholas the Wonder Worker, and she used to have her coachman flogged. He used to weep in my stall and I learned that tears have a pleasant, salty taste. Then the old woman died. Her steward took me to the country and sold me to a hawker. Then I over-ate myself with wheat and grew still worse. They sold me to a peasant. There I ploughed, and had hardly anything to eat, my foot got cut by a ploughshare, and I again became ill. Then a gypsy took me in exchange for something. He tormented me terribly and finally sold me to the steward here. And here I am."

All were silent. A sprinkling of rain began to fall.

I X

The Evening After

As the herd returned home the following evening they encountered their master with a visitor. Zhuldyba when nearing the house looked askance at the two male figures: One was the young master in his straw hat, the other a tall, stout, bloated military man. The old mare gave the man a side glance and, swerving, went near him; the others, the young ones, were flustered and hesitated, especially when the master and his visitor purposely stepped among them, pointing something out to each other and talking.

"That one, the dapple grey, I bought of Voekov," said the master. "And where did you get that young black mare with the white legs?"

"She's a fine one!" said the visitor. They looked over many of the horses going forward and stopping them. They noticed the chestnut filly too.

"That is one I kept of Khrenova's saddle-horse breed," said the master.

They could not see all the horses as they walked past, and the master called to Nester, and the old man, tapping the sides of the piebald with his heels, trotted forward. The piebald limped on one leg but moved in a way that showed that as long as his strength lasted he would not murmur on any account, even if they wanted him to run in that way to the end of the world. He was even ready to gallop and tried to do so with his right leg.

"There, I can say for certain there is no better horse in Russia than this one," said the master, pointing to one of the mares. The visitor admired it. The master walked about excitedly, ran forward, and showed his visitor all the horses, mentioning the origin and pedigree of each. The visitor evidently found the master's talk dull but devised some questions to show interest.

"Yes, yes," he said absent-mindedly.

"Just look," said the master, not answering a question. "Look at her legs. . . . She cost me a lot but has a third foal already in harness."

"And trots well?" asked the guest.

So they went past all the horses till there were no more to show. Then they were silent. "Well, shall we go now?"

"Yes, let's go."

They went through the gate. The visitor was glad the exhibition was over and that he could now go to the house where they could eat and drink and smoke, and he grew perceptibly brighter. As he went past Nester, who sat on the piebald waiting for orders, the visitor slapped the piebald's crupper with his big fat hand.

"What an ornamented one!" he said. "I once had a piebald like him; do you remember my telling you of him?"

The master, finding that it was not his horse that was being spoken about, paid no attention but kept looking round at his own herd.

Suddenly above his ear he heard a dull, weak, senile neigh. It was the piebald tht had begun to neigh and had broken off as if ashamed.

Neither the visitor nor the master paid any attention to this neighing, but went into the house.

In the flabby old man Strider had recognized his beloved master, the once brilliant, handsome, and wealthy Serpukhovskoy.

X

It kept on drizzling. In the stable-yard it was gloomy, but in the master's house it was very different. The table was laid in a luxurious drawing room for a luxurious evening tea, and at it sat the host, the hostess, and their guest.

The hostess, her pregnancy made very noticeable by her figure, her strained convex pose, her plumpness, and especially by her large eyes with their mild inward look, sat by the samovar.

The host held in his hand a box of special, ten-year-old cigars, such as he said no one else had, and he was preparing to boast about them to his guest. The host was a handsome man of about twenty-five, fresh-looking, well cared for, and well groomed. In the house he was wearing a new loose thick suit made in London. Large expensive pendants hung from his watch-chain. His gold-mounted turquoise shirt studs were also large and massive. He had a beard *à la* Napoleon III, and the tips of his moustache stuck out in a way that could only have been learned in Paris.

The hostess wore a dress of silk gauze with a large floral pattern of many colors, and large gold hairpins of a peculiar pattern held up her thick, light-brown hair—beautiful though not all her own. On her arms and hands she wore many bracelets and rings, all of them expensive.

The tea service was of delicate china and the samovar of silver. A footman, resplendent in dress coat, white waistcoat and necktie, stood like a statue

by the door awaiting orders. The furniture was ele-
gantly carved and upholstered in bright colors, the
wallpaper dark with a large flowered pattern. Beside
the table, tinkling the silver bells on its collar, was a
particularly fine whippet, whose difficult English
name its owners, neither of whom knew English,
pronounced.

In the corner, surrounded by plants, stood an in-
laid piano. Everything gave the impression of new-
ness, luxury, and rarity. Everything was good, but it
all bore an imprint of superfluity, wealth, and the absence of intellectual interests.

The host, a lover of trotting races, was sturdy and
full-blooded—one of that never-dying race which
drives about in sable coats, throws expensive bouquets
to actresses, drinks the most expensive wines with the
most fashionable labels at the most expensive restau-
rants, offers prizes engraved with the donor's name,
and keeps the most expensive mistresses.

Nikita Serpukhovskoy, their guest, was a man of
over forty, tall, stout, bald-headed, with heavy moustache and whiskers. He must once have been very
handsome but had now evidently sunk physically,
morally, and financially.

He had such debts that he had been obliged to
enter the government service to avoid imprison-
ment for debt and was now on his way to a provin-

cial town to become the head of a stud farm, a post some important relatives had obtained for him.

He wore a military coat and blue trousers of a kind only a rich man would have had made for himself. His shirt was of similar quality and so was his English watch. His boots had wonderful soles as thick as a man's finger.

Nikita Serpukhovskoy had during his life run through a fortune of two million rubles, and was now a hundred and twenty thousand in debt. In cases of that kind there always remains a certain momentum of life enabling a man to obtain credit and continue living almost luxuriously for another ten years.

These ten years were however coming to an end, the momentum was exhausted, and life was growing hard for Nikita. He was already beginning to drink—that is, to get fuddled with wine, a thing that used not to happen, though strictly speaking he had never begun or left off drinking. His decline was most noticeable in the restlessness of his glance (his eyes had grown shifty) and in the uncertainty of his voice and movements. This restlessness struck one the more as it had evidently got hold of him only recently, for one could see that he had all his life been accustomed not to be afraid of anything or anybody and had only recently, through heavy suffering, reached this state of fear so unnatural to him.

His host and hostess noticed this and exchanged glances which showed that they understood one another and were only postponing till bedtime a detailed discussion of the subject, putting up meanwhile with poor Nikita and even showing him attentions.

The sight of his young host's good fortune humiliated Serpukhovskoy, awakening a painful envy in him as he recalled his own irrecoverable past.

"Do you mind my smoking a cigar, Marie?" he asked, addressing the lady in the peculiar tone acquired only by experience—the tone, polite and friendly but not quite respectful, in which men who know the world speak to kept women in contradistinction to wives. Not that he wished to offend her: On the contrary he now wished rather to curry favor with her and with her keeper, though he would on no account have acknowledged the fact to himself. But he was accustomed to speak in that way to such women. He knew she would herself be surprised and even offended were he to treat her as a lady. Besides he had to retain a certain shade of a respectful tone for his friend's real wife. He always treated his friend's mistresses with respect, not because he shared the so-called convictions promulgated in periodicals (he never read trash or that kind) about the respect due to the personality of every man, about the meaninglessness of marriage, and so forth, but because all decent men do so and he was a decent, though fallen, man.

He took a cigar. But his host awkwardly picked up a whole handful and offered them to him.

"Just see how good these are. Take them!"

Serpukhowskoy pushed aside the hand with the cigars, and a gleam of offense and shame showed itself in his eyes.

"Thank you!" He took out his cigar case. "Try mine!"

The hostess was sensitive. She noticed his embarrassment and hastened to talk to him. "I am very fond of cigars. I should smoke myself if everyone about me did not smoke." And she smiled her pretty, kindly smile.

He smiled in return, but irresolutely. Two of his teeth were missing.

"No, take this!" the tactless host continued. "The others are weaker. Fritz, bring another box. There are two there."

The German footman brought another box.

"Do you prefer big ones? Strong ones? These are very good. Take them all!" he continued, forcing them on his guest.

He was evidently glad to have someone to boast to of the rare things he possessed, and he noticed nothing amiss. Serpukhovskoy lit his cigar and hastened to resume the conversation they had begun.

"So, how much did you pay for Atlasny?" he asked.

"He cost me a great deal, not less than five thousand, but at any rate I am already safe on him. What colts he gets, I tell you!"

"Do they trot?" asked Serpukhovskoy.

"They trot well! His colt took three prizes this year: In Tula, in Moscow, and in Petersburg; he raced Voekov's Raven. That rascal, the driver, let him make four false steps or he'd have left the other behind the flag."

"He's a bit green. Too much Dutch blood in him, that's what I say," remarked Serpukhovskoy.

"Well, but what about the mares? I'll show Goody to you tomorrow. I gave three thousand for her. For Amiable I gave two thousand."

And the host again began to enumerate his possessions. The hostess saw that this hurt Serpukhovskoy and that he was only pretending to listen. "Will you have some more tea?" she asked.

"I won't," replied the host and went on talking. She rose, the host stopped her, embraced her, and kissed her.

As he looked at them Serpukhovskoy for their sakes tried to force a smile, but after the host had got up, embraced her, and let her to the *portière,* Serpukhovskoy's face suddenly changed. He sighed heavily, and a look of despair showed itself on his flabby face. Even malevolence appeared on it.

The host returned and smilingly sat down opposite him. They were silent awhile.

XI

"Yes, you were saying you bought him of Voekov," remarked Serpukhovskoy with assumed carelessness.

"Oh, yes, that was of Atlasny, you know. I always meant to buy some mares of Dubovitzki, but he had nothing but rubbish left."

"He has failed. . . . " said Serpukhovskoy, and suddenly stopped and glanced round. He remembered that he owed that bankrupt twenty thousand rubles, and if it came to talking of being bankrupt it was certainly said that he was one. He laughed.

Both again sat silent for a long time. The host considered what he could brag about to his guest. Serpukhovskoy was thinking what he could say to show that he did not consider himself bankrupt. But the minds of both worked with difficulty, in spite of efforts to brace themselves up with cigars.

"When are we going to have a drink?" thought Serpukhovskoy.

"I must certainly have a drink or I shall die of ennui with this fellow," thought the host.

"Will you be remaining here long?" Serpukhovskoy asked.

"Another month. Well, shall we have supper, eh? Fritz, is it ready?"

They went into the dining room. There under a hanging lamp stood a table on which were candles and all sorts of extraordinary things: syphons, and little dolls fastened to corks, rare wine in decanters, unusual hors-d'oeuvres, and vodka. They had a drink, ate a little, drank again, ate again, and their conversation got into swing. Serpukhovskoy was flushed and began to speak without timidity.

They spoke of women and of who kept this one or that, a gypsy, a ballet girl, or a Frenchwoman.

"And have you given up Mathieu?" asked the host. That was the woman who had ruined Serpukhovskoy.

"No, she left me. Ah, my dear fellow, when I recall what I have got through in my life! Now I am really glad when I have a thousand rubles, and am glad to get away from everybody. I can't stand it in Moscow. But what's the good of talking!"

The host found it tiresome to listen to Serpukhovskoy. He wanted to speak about himself—to brag. But Serpukhovskoy also wished to talk about himself, about his brilliant past. His host filled his glass for him and waited for him to stop, so that he might tell him about himself and how his stud was now arranged as no one had ever had a stud arranged before. And that Marie loved him with her heart and not merely for his wealth.

"I wanted to tell you that in my stud. . . . " he began, but Serpukhovskoy interrupted him.

"I may say that there was a time," Serpukhovskoy began, "when I liked to live well and knew how to do it. Now you talk about trotting—tell me which is your fastest horse."

The host, glad of an opportunity to tell more about his stud, was beginning, when Serpukhovskoy again interrupted him.

"Yes, yes," he said, "but you breeders do it just out of vanity and not for pleasure, not for the joy of life. It was different with me. You know I told you I had a driving horse, a piebald with just the same kind of spots as the one your keeper was riding. Oh, what a horse that was! You can't possibly know: it was in 1842, when I had just come to Moscow; I went to a horse dealer and there I saw a well-bred piebald gelding. I liked him. The price? One thousand rubles. I liked him, so I took him and began to drive with him. I never had, and you have not and never will have, such a horse. I never knew one like him for speed and for strength. You were a boy then and couldn't have known, but you may have heard of him. All Moscow was talking about him."

"Yes, I heard of him," the host unwillingly replied. "But what I wished to say about mine. . . ."

"Ah, then you did hear! I bought him just as he was, without pedigree and without a certificate; it was only afterwards that I got to know Voekov and found out. He was a colt by Affable I. Strider—because of his long strides. On account of his piebald spots he was removed from the Khrenova stud and given to the head keeper, who had him castrated and sold him to the horse dealer. There are no such horses now, my dear chap. Ah, those were the days! Ah, vanished youth!" And he sang the words of the gypsy song. He was getting tipsy. "Ah, those were the good times. I was twenty-five and had eighty thousand rubles a year, not a single grey hair, and all my teeth like pearls. . . . Whatever I touched succeeded, and now it is all ended. . . . "

"But there was not the same mettlesomeness then," said the host, availing himself of the pause. "Let me tell you that my first horses began to trot without . . ."

"Your horses! But they used to be more mettlesome . . ."

"How—more mettlesome?"

"Yes, more mettlesome! I remember as if it were today how I drove him once to the trotting races in Moscow. No horse of mine was running. I did not care for trotters, mine were thoroughbreds: General

Chaulet, Mahomet. I drove up with my piebald. My driver was a fine fellow, I was fond of him, but he also took to drink. . . . Well, so I got there."

" 'Serpukhovskoy,' I was asked, 'When are you going to keep trotters?' 'The devil take your lubbers!' I replied. 'I have a piebald hack that can outpace all your trotters!' 'Oh no, he won't!' 'I'll bet a thousand rubles!' Agreed, and they started. He came in five seconds ahead and I won the thousand rubles. But what of it? I did a little over sixty-six miles in three hours with a troyka of thoroughbreds. All Moscow knows it."

And Serpukhovskoy began to brag so glibly and continuously that his host could not get a single word in and sat opposite him with a dejected countenance, filling up his own and his guest's glass every now and then by way of distraction.

The dawn was breaking and still they sat there. It became intolerably dull for the host. He got up.

"If we are to go to bed, let's go!" said Serpukhovskoy rising, and reeling and puffing, he went to the room prepared for him.

The host was lying beside his mistress. "No, he is unendurable," he said. "He gets drunk and swaggers incessantly."

"And he makes up to me."

"I'm afraid he'll be asking for money."

Serpukhovskoy was lying on the bed in his clothes, breathing heavily.

"I must have been lying a lot," he thought. "Well, no matter! The wine was good, but he is an awful swine. There's something cheap about him. And I'm an awful swine," he said to himself and laughed aloud. "First I used to keep women and now I'm kept. Yes, the Winkler girl will support me. I take money of her. Serves him right. Still, I must undress. Can't get my boots off. Hullo! Hullo!" he called out, but the man who had been told off to wait on him had long since gone to bed.

He sat down, took off his coat and waistcoat and somehow managed to kick off his trousers, but for a long time could not get his boots off—his soft stomach being in the way. He got one off at last, and struggled for a long time with the other, panting and becoming exhausted. And so with his foot in the boot-top he rolled over and began to snore, filling the room with a smell of tobacco, wine, and disagreeable old age.

XII

If Strider recalled anything that night, he was distracted by Vaska, who threw a rug over him, galloped off on him, and kept him standing till morning at the door of a tavern, near a peasant horse. They licked one another. In the morning when Strider returned to the herd he kept rubbing himself.

Five days passed. They called in a veterinary, who said cheerfully: "It's the itch; let me sell him to the gypsies."

"What's the use? Cut his throat, and get it done today."

The morning was calm and clear. The herd went to pasture, but Strider was left behind. A strange man came—thin, dark, and dirty, in a coat splashed with something black. It was the knacker. Without looking at Strider he took him by the halter they had put on him and led him away. Strider went quietly without looking round, dragging along as usual and catching his hind feet in the straw.

When they were out of the gate he strained towards the well, but the knacker jerked his halter, saying: "Not worth while."

The knacker and Vaska, who followed behind, went to a hollow behind the brick barn and stopped as if there were something peculiar about this very ordinary place. The knacker, handing the halter to Vaska, took off his coat, rolled up his sleeves, and produced a knife and a whetstone from his boot leg. The gelding stretched towards the halter meaning to chew it a little from dullness, but he could not reach it. He sighed and closed his eyes. His nether lip hung down, disclosing his worn yellow teeth, and he began to drowse to the sound of the sharpening of the knife. Only his swollen, aching, outstretched leg kept jerking. Suddenly he felt himself being taken by the lower jaw and his head lifted. He opened his eyes. There were two dogs in front of him; one was sniffing at the knacker, the other was sitting and watching the gelding as if expecting something from him. The gelding looked at them and began to rub his jaw against the arm that was holding him.

"Want to doctor me probably—well, let them!" he thought.

And in fact he felt that something had been done to his throat. It hurt, and he shuddered and gave a kick with one foot, but restrained himself and waited for what would follow. . . . Then he felt something liquid streaming down his neck and chest. He heaved a profound sigh and felt much better. The whole burden of his life was eased.

He closed his eyes and began to droop his head. No one was holding it. Then his legs quivered and his whole body swayed. He was not so much frightened as surprised.

Everything was so new to him. He was surprised and started forward and upward, but instead of this, in moving from the spot his legs got entangled, he began to fall sideways, and trying to take a step fell forward and down on his left side.

The knacker waited till the convulsions had ceased, drove away the dogs that had crept nearer, took the gelding by the legs, turned him on his back, told Vaska to hold a leg, and began to skin the horse.

"It was a horse, too," remarked Vaska.

"If he had been better fed, the skin would have been fine," said the knacker.

The herd returned downhill in the evening, and those on the left saw down below something red, round which dogs were busy and above which hawks and crows were flying. One of the dogs, pressing its paws against the carcass and swinging his head, with a crackling sound tore off what it had seized hold of. The chestnut filly stopped, stretched out her head and neck, and sniffed the air for a long time. They could hardly drive her away.

At dawn, in a ravine of the old forest, down in an overgrown glade, big-headed wolf cubs were howling joyfully. There were five of them: four almost alike and one with a head bigger than his body. A lean old wolf who was shedding her coat, dragging her full belly with its hanging dugs along the ground, came out of the bushes and sat down in front of the cubs. The cubs came and stood round her in a semicircle. She went to the smallest, and bending her knee and holding her muzzle down, made some convulsive movements, and opening her large sharp-toothed jaws disgorged a large piece of horseflesh. The bigger cubs rushed towards her, but she moved threateningly at them and let the little one have it all. The little one, growling as if in anger, pulled the horseflesh under him and began to gorge. In the same way the mother wolf coughed up a piece for the second, the third, and all five of them, and then lay down in front of them to rest.

A week later only a large skull and two shoulder blades lay behind the barn; the rest had all been taken away. In summer a peasant, collecting bones, carried away these shoulder blades and skull and put them to use.

The dead body of Serpukhovskoy, which had walked about the earth eating and drinking, was put under ground much later. Neither his skin, nor his flesh, nor his bones, were of any use.

Just as for the last twenty years his body that had walked the earth had been a great burden to everybody, so the putting away of that body was again an additional trouble to people. He had not been wanted by anybody for a long time and had only been a burden, yet the dead who bury their dead found it necessary to clothe that swollen body, which at once began to decompose, in a good uniform and good boots and put it into a new and expensive coffin with tassels at its four corners, and then to place that coffin in another coffin of lead, to take it to Moscow and there dig up some long buried human bones, and to hide in that particular spot this decomposing maggoty body in its new uniform and polished boots, and cover it all up with earth.

IF YOU LIKED THIS BOOK, DON'T MISS THESE OTHER LYONS TITLES.

THE GREATEST HORSE STORIES EVER TOLD by Steven D. Price

SOME HORSES by Tom McGuane

THE FARAWAY HORSES by Buck Brannaman

HORSES AND OTHER HEROES by Don Burt

THE QUOTABLE HORSE LOVER by Steven D. Price

THE SPORTING LIFE by Bill Barich

FORWARD MOTION by Holly Menino

STRAIGHT WEST by Lindy Smith and Verlyn Klinkenborg